THE

Sanctity of Marriage

H A N D B O O K

# THE
# Sanctity of Marriage
# HANDBOOK

The Ultimate Guide to Marriage
*—Between a Man and a Woman—*
Featuring
Those Who Cast the First Stone

## Bryan Harris

Jeremy P. Tarcher/Penguin
*a member of Penguin Group (USA) Inc.*
*New York*

JEREMY P. TARCHER/PENGUIN
Published by the Penguin Group
Penguin Group (USA) Inc., 375 Hudson Street, New York,
New York 10014, USA • Penguin Group (Canada), 90 Eglinton Avenue East, Suite 700, Toronto,
Ontario M4P 2Y3, Canada (a division of Pearson Penguin Canada Inc.) • Penguin Books Ltd, 80
Strand, London WC2R 0RL, England • Penguin Ireland, 25 St Stephen's Green, Dublin 2, Ireland (a
division of Penguin Books Ltd) • Penguin Group (Australia), 250 Camberwell Road, Camberwell,
Victoria 3124, Australia (a division
of Pearson Australia Group Pty Ltd) • Penguin Books India Pvt Ltd, 11 Community Centre,
Panchsheel Park, New Delhi–110 017, India • Penguin Group (NZ), Cnr Airborne and Rosedale
Roads, Albany, Auckland 1310, New Zealand (a division
of Pearson New Zealand Ltd) • Penguin Books (South Africa) (Pty) Ltd,
24 Sturdee Avenue, Rosebank, Johannesburg 2196, South Africa

Penguin Books Ltd, Registered Offices:
80 Strand, London WC2R 0RL, England

Most Tarcher/Penguin books are available at special quantity discounts for bulk purchase for sales
promotions, premiums, fund-raising, and educational needs. Special books or book excerpts also
can be created to fit specific needs. For details, write Penguin Group (USA) Inc. Special Markets, 375
Hudson Street, New York, NY 10014.

Library of Congress Cataloging-in-Publication Data

Harris, Bryan, date.
The sanctity of marriage handbook : the ultimate guide to marriage—between a man and a
woman—featuring those who cast the first stone /
Bryan Harris.
p. cm.
Includes bibliographical references.
ISBN 1-58542-449-8
1. Conservatism—United States.   2. Politicians—United States—Conduct of life.
3. Politicians—United States—Family relationships.   4. Marriage law—United States.   5. Social
values—United States.   6. Hypocrisy.   I. Title.
JC573.2.U6H37   2005                       2005048569
320.53'092'273—dc22

Printed in the United States of America
1   3   5   7   9   10   8   6   4   2

Book design by Stephanie Huntwork

# CONTENTS

## The Silent Majority

## Self-Loathers and Wily Evaders

## (Dis) Honorable Mentions

# DIVORCE RATES OF U.S. STATES

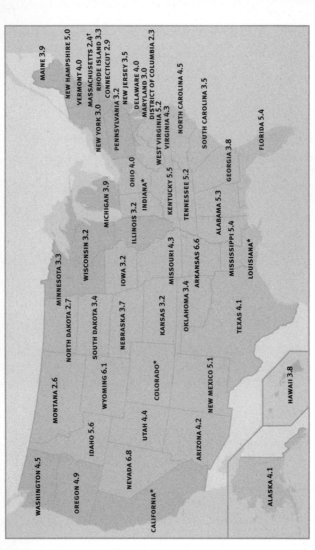

WASHINGTON 4.5
OREGON 4.9
IDAHO 5.6
MONTANA 2.6
NORTH DAKOTA 2.7
MINNESOTA 3.3
WISCONSIN 3.2
MICHIGAN 3.9
MAINE 3.9
NEW HAMPSHIRE 5.0
VERMONT 4.0
MASSACHUSETTS 2.4†
RHODE ISLAND 3.3
CONNECTICUT 2.9
NEW YORK 3.0
PENNSYLVANIA 3.2
NEW JERSEY 3.5
DELAWARE 4.0
MARYLAND 3.0
DISTRICT OF COLUMBIA 2.3
WEST VIRGINIA 5.2
VIRGINIA 4.3
NORTH CAROLINA 4.5
SOUTH CAROLINA 3.5
OHIO 4.0
INDIANA*
ILLINOIS 3.2
IOWA 3.2
SOUTH DAKOTA 3.4
WYOMING 6.1
UTAH 4.4
COLORADO*
NEVADA 6.8
CALIFORNIA*
ARIZONA 4.2
NEW MEXICO 5.1
NEBRASKA 3.7
KANSAS 3.2
OKLAHOMA 3.4
MISSOURI 4.3
ARKANSAS 6.6
KENTUCKY 5.5
TENNESSEE 5.2
ALABAMA 5.3
MISSISSIPPI 5.4
LOUISIANA*
GEORGIA 3.8
FLORIDA 5.4
TEXAS 4.1
HAWAII 3.8
ALASKA 4.1

AVERAGE DIVORCE RATES IN RED STATES, EXCLUDING COLORADO, INDIANA, AND LOUISIANA: 4.3
AVERAGE DIVORCE RATES IN BLUE STATES, EXCLUDING CALIFORNIA: 3.5

*U.S. CENSUS DATA FOR 2001 WAS NOT AVAILABLE FOR CALIFORNIA, COLORADO, INDIANA, AND LOUISIANA.
†LOWEST IN THE UNITED STATES

This nation is like all the others that have been spewed upon the earth—ready to shout for any cause that will tickle its vanity or fill its pocket. What a hell of a heaven it will be when they get all these hypocrites assembled there!

—*Mark Twain, letter to J. H. Twichell,*
*January 29, 1901*

## INTRODUCTION

## Only You Can Prevent Gay Marriage

**I**T'S THE CLASSIC love story gone wrong.

Back in 2000, a pair of suitors came knocking on America's collective electoral door. One was brainy, but not very sexy, slightly wooden, with tree-hugging tendencies and a penchant for overstating his contributions to the Internet revolution. He wanted America's heart. The other was a hick from the backwoods (read: Midland, Texas) whose twang and malapropisms charmed the pants off everyone, and he had a couple coins to rub together, a nice car, and some influential friends and family members. He wasn't interested in anything serious—just wanted to test the waters, see if America would put out before his first term was over. But it was Gore who scored, not Bush—or he thought he had until the Supreme Court intervened. America put up a fight, but, succumbing to peer pressure (bullying brother, witchy attorney general, corporate-controlled media, TV "experts" awarding states to the hick before the polls had closed), finally gave it up to Bush. It wasn't long before the union was sanctified by the hick's family friends, the Supreme Court. Now America is the old ball-and-chain, and Bush is busy chasing tail in Iraq.

The union between George W. Bush and the United States of America isn't the country's only bad marriage. In fact, according to the latest U.S. census data, nearly half of all marriages end in divorce. *Half.* And yet it remains a decidedly sacred institution, one so hallowed that in twenty-six states you can marry your cousin. It is such a holy union that you can be married by someone who has been ordained via the Internet. Marriage is so sacrosanct and sturdy that many participants prefer the "open" variety.

But to hear tell from extreme right-wingers, the venerable institution of marriage, one resilient enough to withstand Britney Spears, Henry VIII, and Liza Minnelli, is on the verge of disappearance if same-sex marriage is not prevented through a constitutional amendment. And their infallible logic underscores this point: many opponents of same-sex marriage claim the only purpose of marriage is procreation. A valid reason for discrimination, they argue, is that there is a legitimate purpose for the government to promote an "optimal social structure for the bearing and raising of children."

Okay, that works. But only, as Dahlia Lithwick of *Slate* points out, if you also oppose childlessness by choice, birth control, "living in sin," and postmenopause marriage. Oh, and if you're talking "optimal social structure," Lithwick argues, you gotta get rid of those single parents, poor folk, alcoholics, terminally ill parents, and other people who have a hard row to hoe.

But let's not beat around the Bush: all this talk of family values and morality is one sloppy euphemism for antigay legislation. After all, it's the gays who have been most successfully subverting America's moral path, right? They and their attorneys have conspired to twist the Constitutional definitions of civil rights for the sake of their own deplorable ends. (Republicans, on the other hand, would never do such a thing.) They have made a mockery of marriage, an institution that hundreds of conservative legislators are willing to go to any lengths to keep for themselves. How dare the gays try to publicly commit to a loving, monogamous, long-term union! There is simply no room in a moral-loving country for that kind of "selfish hedonism" (with apologies to Alan Keyes).

Sarcasm aside, it's true that the right wing is judging the rest of humanity based on a standard that they themselves cannot even uphold. This little book details the hypocrisy of the right wing's "sanctity of marriage" dogma by profiling some of the right wing's most vocal "defenders"—and legislators— of marriage, and seeing just how well they live up to that sacred ideal.

Consider Bob Barr, a true culture warrior, who penned the Defense of Marriage Act. And why shouldn't he have? He was a senior member of Congress, one with considerable war experience and battle scars—no, not from any foreign war (he, like so many other right-wing politicians, managed to opt out of military service) but from the never-ending domestic war. He's been married three times. Then there's Alan Keyes, a deeply dedicated family man and noted Christian, calling his lesbian daughter (and Mary Cheney) "selfish hedonists," then disowning her. Architect of the Contract with America and Grand Wizard of the Clinton lynch mob, Newt Gingrich is a shining beacon of marital responsibility, divorcing his wife as she lay in a hospital bed recovering from cancer, and getting blow jobs on the side (a mental image almost as hard to erase from the psyche as that of Bill O'Reilly coming at you with a soapy loofah sponge).

But wait a minute—we handed over the reins of the country to these sorts of fellas because they told us that they were all about family values. Perhaps we never bothered to ask just what exactly those family values were.

Despite the hypocrisy demonstrated by the subjects of this book—folks who grab the Bible with one hand and play grab-ass with the other—this is not just a book about hypocrites. It is about people who cultivate hate, who, oftentimes, *legislate* it, and then disguise it as being for the good of all. Consider for a moment the fact that we are on the brink of becoming the first American generation in history to alter the Constitution of the United States in order to *take rights away* from our own citizens.

It's not a stretch to liken Strom Thurmond's support of Jim Crow to George W. Bush's fight against gay rights. See, Jim Crow didn't oppress blacks, it protected "friendly relations" between the races that existed under those laws. And George W. Bush isn't about depriving gays and lesbians of equal opportunity—he is merely "protecting America's religious and natural roots without weakening the good influence of society" (whatever the hell that syntactical nightmare means).

The Thurmond/Bush method paid off in 2004. Bush's reelection hinged on a few hundred thousand votes. Über-Christian political megalith Dr. James Dobson told *Christianity Today* that Bush's stand on gay marriage mobilized the religious right:

> There's no question that the effort to protect marriage certainly helped to energize and engage many Christians in the election process. I have been critical in the past of the church's reluctance to "dirty itself" in these so-called politi-

cal battles, which are in reality profoundly moral in nature, but I believe this signals the dawn of a new day.

In the past decade, the same-sex marriage saga has played itself out in two acts: Act One began in 1993, when the Hawaii Supreme Court found same-sex marriage to be legal, overturning lower court findings.

The next year the Republican class of '94 stormed Congress clutching the Contract with America in their greasy little palms, and stowing a shiny new "family values" social agenda in their backpacks, pulled out mainly during reelection campaigns. The Republicans established a congressional majority for the first time in decades and, two years later, wrote the Defense of Marriage Act, which defined marriage as a union between a man and a woman.

Once marriage was federally safe and sound, the Compassionate Conservatives started on President Clinton (the same President Clinton who signed the Defense of Marriage Act). The impeachment proceeding was a tent revival of epic proportions, with stand-up guys as varied as Dan Burton, Newt Gingrich, Henry Hyde, and more, loudly condemning Clinton for philandering and lying, two things they could never condone.

Except that they did it all the time.

It's a sad commentary on the Left that the journalist who brought the hypocrisy of the Right out in the open was *Hustler* publisher Larry Flynt. Flynt put a bounty on the bawdy secrets of the "moral majority." A tidal wave of revelations (and not the biblical kind) overtook the Hill, including adulterous affairs, multiple divorces, illegitimate children, and numerous financial improprieties. The Clinton impeachment ended in a censure, and left as much mud on the prosecutors as on the president. All was fairly quiet, and it seemed as if the phony moralists had been humbled.

But then in 2004, a funny thing happened on the way to the Massachusetts Supreme Court. Act Two opened with a bang: the state Supreme Court deemed same-sex marriage constitutional in Massachusetts. Within hours of the news, cities around the United States began to issue marriage licenses to same-sex couples.

Republicans acted swiftly. President George W. Bush publicly asked for an amendment to the 218-year-old document that preserved life, liberty, and the pursuit of happiness for citizens of the United States—a document that had been amended in the past to enlarge those rights for African-Americans and women, among others—to deny the right of marriage to gays.

The Repubs got right on it, made wiser by their missteps during the Clinton impeachment. The bill's sponsors were less shifty characters: Senator Wayne Allard and Representative Marilyn Musgrave, both from Colorado.

One might think with all its liberal "activist" judges and all the bleeding hearts that Congress recently stepped on, Massachusetts would have a divorce rate that echoed its noninterventionist interpretation of marriage. Not so. Massachusetts has the lowest divorce rate per capita in the entire country, at 2.4 divorces per 1,000 residents. The divorce rate in Texas is twice that (and hey, we're even giving the conservatives the benefit of the doubt here, using statistics from the Barna Research Group, an ultra-right-wing research company headed by a born-again Christian). Consider the following statistics:

- Born-again Christians are among the most divorced group in the country.
- According to the U.S. Census, divorce is most prevalent in the so-called Bible Belt.
- The divorce rates in notable red states (Alabama, Texas, Georgia, North Carolina, Mississippi, Oklahoma, Arkansas, Florida, and South Carolina) are about 50 percent higher than the national average.
- The divorce rates in notable blue states (New York, Rhode Island, Connecticut, Maine, New Hampshire, Pennsylvania, Vermont, Massachusetts, New Jersey) are the lowest in the country.

This book profiles the men and women who have won seats in Congress and won the hearts (and votes) of evangelicals across the country, the media pundits who have saturated the radio and television airwaves with their hypocrisy, and the telegenic religious leaders who have cast judgment on millions by saying on television and in print that gays have made a mockery of the sacred institution of marriage, an institution that thousands of committed right-wing legislators are willing to go to any lengths to defend so they can partake of it again and again (and again).

Blowhards

*I*N THIS HANDBOOK of the hell-bound, there are few better poised to lead by example than this band of brothers (and sisters), an angry army of red-faced politicians and pundits defending an institution that they want to keep to themselves so they can tap its ass anytime they want—sometimes three or four times. The vision of America these people promote is an exclusionary enclave where those granted the right to marry are those most likely to desecrate the institution. But at least they're straight.

There's a line in the Good Book that these Bible-thumpers don't trot out that often: *By their fruits you shall know them.* If we did as all these blowhards do, America would look not like June Cleaver's well-kept home but, rather, more like David Koresh's compound: we'd all be armed to the teeth, sleeping on piles of mistresses, and spouting our own cracked-out, self-serving interpretations of the Bible.

Those profiled in this section were categorized as "blowhards" if they condemned same-sex marriage, voted for the Defense of Marriage Act and/or supported the Federal Marriage Amendment to the Constitution, ran their election campaigns on a "family values" or "morality" platform, and, in some cases, if they worked overtime to bring down a phi-landering president for his "moral failures" while they them-selves were busy winking, nodding, and chasing tail—all the while proving that the moral authority of the right wing is as much a put-on as George W. Bush's flight suit.

# Representative Bob Barr

## (R·GEORGIA, RETIRED)

### Author of the Defense of Marriage Act

The very foundations of our society are in danger of being burned. The flames of hedonism, the flames of narcissism, the flames of self-centered morality are licking at the very foundations of our society: the family unit.

—*Bob Barr on same-sex marriage*

## His Remarkable Career

Bob Barr represented the Seventh District of Georgia in the U.S. House of Representatives from 1995 to 2003, where he served as a senior member of the House Judiciary Committee. Representative Barr's most significant contribution to the religious right was his 1996 Defense of Marriage Act, which, when signed into law by President Bill Clinton, a man Barr attacks to this day for his moral failings, effectively put a federal ban on same-sex marriage. Barr famously called hate-crimes legislation designed to protect the rights of gays, lesbians, women, and disabled citizens a "back door way to obtain protected status for sexual orientation and sexual deviancy." Barr, author of the syntactically challenged book *The Meaning of Is: The Squandered Impeachment and Wasted Legacy of William Jefferson Clinton,* is a wunderkind of morality and family values, claiming that the institution of marriage is sacred, that its foundation in American society, while deep and firm, is threatened by the very idea of legalizing unions between gays who wish to consecrate their own partnerships. It is an institution to protect, Barr has said, and he will defend it from those who would defile it.

Which begs the question: which marriage is Barr defending? He has his choice: his first marriage, his second, or his third.

## His Personal Commitment

Champion of the National Rifle Association (NRA) and sweetheart of the "family values" crowd, ol' Bob has been married three times and been sued for child support. In 1992, he showed his support for the foundations of our society by licking whipped cream from the cleavages of two women at a leukemia fundraiser. When confronted with the photographs of this principled act, Representative Barr said it had been done for charitable reasons—his table had donated two hundred dollars to the cause and so he ran his tongue over the breasts of a credit-card executive and a nurse.

The flames of hedonism, indeed.

Let's fast-forward to the details of Barr's moral fortitude and sexual propriety, as evidenced in the legal fallout of his second sanctified coupling.

As a leading torch bearer in the Clinton lynch mob, Barr became a target of *Hustler* publisher Larry Flynt's notorious campaign to unveil Republican moral hypocrisy. In an affidavit to *Hustler,* Barr's second wife, Gail, a former CIA analyst, said Barr consented to and paid for her 1983 abortion. She later came to realize, when filling in for Barr's secretary, that she was scheduling lunches for him with his mistress and soon-to-be third wife, Jeri Dobbin. When questioned under oath about his "meetings" with Jeri, which took place while Barr was still married to Gail, the righteous congressman would not dignify the accusations with a comment. (Read: he neither denied nor confirmed the charge, claiming possible self-incrimination—a principle of privacy that Barr did not extend to Bill Clinton. And, in a hilariously ironic twist, Barr currently occupies the 21st Century Liberties Chair for Freedom and Privacy and the American Conservative Union.) Barr couldn't dignify the accusations with comment, it seems, because he was too busy writing the Defense of Marriage Act.

Yet in Gail Barr's affidavit, she stated that Bob, ever the attentive husband, refused to stop campaigning while she went through treatment for breast cancer, despite her pleas. "He never went to the chemotherapy treatments with me,"

Gail stated. "He was not there when I needed him." Gail's affidavit also reports that on Thanksgiving of 1986, Barr left his wife and two boys, telling Gail, "I don't love you anymore." When she asked him to stay through the holiday for the sake of the boys, he refused, and drove straight to Jeri's apartment, where he began living.

The flames of self-centered morality, indeed.

But it was a heterosexual marriage, nonetheless, and this loving union was sacred, protected by the state, and protected by Barr from those who would improve it. And despite his spotty track record when it comes to the sanctity of marriage, the Christian Coalition consistently gives him a 100 percent rating. (Incidentally, Barr married Jeri one month after his divorce to Gail became final.)

After constituents aborted him in 2002, Barr now peddles his morality secondhand in speeches across the country.

---

### MORALITY SCORE

**Marriages: three. Divorces: two.
Abortions: one. Charitable acts: one.
Accusations of an affair that went
undignified without a response: one.**

# Representative Newt Gingrich

## FORMER SPEAKER OF THE HOUSE

### (R-Georgia)

## His Remarkable Career

In 1943, an unmarried Pennsylvania teenager gave birth to a baby boy she named Newton, or "little Newt." Nearly fifty years later, Representative Newt Gingrich would engineer the Contract with America, a Republican agenda that united the party and helped it gain a Congressional majority for the first time in forty years. Among the first items of business: deny welfare to single mothers.

Gingrich received a degree from Emory University, and later took his master's and doctorate in modern European history from Tulane University. Before becoming the representative for Georgia's Sixth District in 1978, Gingrich taught history and environmental studies at West Georgia

College, with no documented Dick Armey-esque escapades (see page 46).

In 1995, the same year Gingrich was named *Time* magazine's Man of the Year, he was elected Speaker of the House. During his tenure as Speaker, Gingrich took credit for passing the first balanced budget "in a generation," as he would later crow on his Web site, Newt.org, as well as the alleged first tax cut in sixteen years. Nine of the ten provisions Gingrich had written into the Contract with America were passed into law.

In addition to his legislative activities, Gingrich found time to write and publish seven books, including *Contract with America, To Renew America, Saving Lives & Saving Money,* and his most recent pre-presidential-bid potboiler: *Winning the Future: A 21st Century Contract with America.*

## His Personal Commitment

Always the teacher's pet, Newt Gingrich married his former high school geometry teacher, Jackie Battley, at the ripe old age of nineteen. Six years later, he had an affair with a married woman named Anne Manning. Or had "relations" with Anne Manning (sexual nomenclature would come into play during Gingrich's years as a Speaker of the House, presiding over impeachment proceedings notorious for a brand of confused diction Gingrich himself favors).

"We had oral sex," Manning revealed to *Vanity Fair*. "He prefers that modus operandi because then he can say, 'I never slept with her.'" This M.O. was later christened "The Newt Defense," one used by husbands across the country.

Gingrich's oral dalliance either went unnoticed or was forgiven by Jackie Battley, because their marriage lasted for another four years. In 1981, as she was receiving cancer treatment in a hospital room, the two Gingrich children by her side, Gingrich walked in with a yellow legal pad and asked her for a divorce. A few months later, he married a woman named Marianne Ginther.

By the time he was being lauded as the savior of the Republican Party, the champion of family values—a platform he campaigned on—and *Time*'s Man of the Year, Gingrich was "fooling around with his girl on the Hill," as the *New York Post* revealed. The girl on the Hill was a thirty-three-year-old congressional aide named Callista Bisek. Gingrich, a man who once railed against Democrats for having "Woody Allen family values," was still married to and living with Marianne in their Washington apartment while he was using Bisek as his "frequent breakfast companion," as reported by Gail Sheehy in *Vanity Fair*. Hill aides reported to *Salon* that the lovebirds' breakfast venue of choice was the

Supreme Court cafeteria, across the street from Gingrich's apartment.

And yet, things weren't all roses and blow jobs for the Speaker; at the same time he was allegedly bedding Bisek, the Federal Election Commission charged him for receiving illegal campaign contributions during the 1990 election from his GOPAC organization. (Although Gingrich denied violating tax laws, he received a Congressional censure—the first Speaker of the House ever convicted by his peers—and was fined $300,000.) It was a bit of a delicate situation, especially since Gingrich had recently been photographed with Bill Clinton in New Hampshire, shaking hands in celebration of their pledge to seek campaign-finance reform.

In 1998, while establishing himself as a firebrand in the Clinton impeachment over blow jobs, Gingrich rejected the resignation of House Judiciary Committee Chairman Henry Hyde (R-Illinois) when *Salon* unearthed Hyde's adulterous past. Simultaneously, Gingrich grew more muted in his criticism of Clinton's indiscretions. Some may have thought Gingrich was finally sporting some of that Christian compassion he was so keen on legislating in the form of antiabortion laws and the yanking of welfare from single moms. But there was a blonde lurking in his closet.

Three tabloids exposed Gingrich's six-year affair with Bisek, a woman twenty-three years Gingrich's junior. The relationship had, sources told *Salon,* been old news on the

Hill. Everybody knew. The Manning affair then came to light, and though Gingrich wouldn't confirm the relationship, he did say that he'd "start with the assumption that all human beings sin. So all I'll say is that I've led a human life."

Human life? Or life of a hypocrite?

The political repercussions of Gingrich's checkered past were great for this frequent Christian Coalition guest speaker. And, unfortunately for Gingrich, being Speaker of the House meant there was nobody in a higher position than he was to reject his resignation, and so Gingrich resigned in January 1999 after Democrats won five more seats in the House of Representatives.

Gingrich served his wife, Marianne, with divorce papers, and Marianne won the right to question Bisek in the divorce proceedings.

On October 18, 1999, *Time* magazine, the very magazine that had named Newt Gingrich Man of the Year in 1995, noted the similarities between Gingrich's indelicate situation and that of the man he would have had impeached for the same offense.

> "You are commanded to produce each and every gift . . . given to you by Defendant."
>
> —*Subpoena received by*
> *Monica Lewinsky in* Jones v. Clinton

"You are commanded to produce any and all gifts received by you from the Plaintiff."

*—Subpoena received by Callista Bisek in Newt Gingrich divorce*

Gingrich married Bisek in 1999. The third Mrs. Gingrich is pictured with her husband on the dust jacket of his latest book, *Winning the Future,* in which he describes a new Contract with America, including the need for more Christian morality in the legislative process.

He never mentions how this Christian morality should apply to legislators who bounce checks and those who bang the staff. The obvious answer would be "badly," but the Lord works in strange ways for men who would, literally, cut federal funding for their own mothers. For a man who gained his position as Speaker of the House of Representatives of the United States by campaigning on family values as he was allegedly cheating on a wife or two, it might not come as any surprise that the divorce rate among conservative Christians—among the most vocal opponents of same-sex marriage—is nearly 30 percent. It may come as a surprise, though (or maybe not), to those supporters of same-sex marriage to hear that Gingrich, of all people, believes that gays are "trying to destroy traditional marriage" by having the audacity to ask that their unions be sanctified. Leave that sanctity stuff up to the experts—the ones who have tried it again and again and again. Those who happen to be homosexual, well, good luck in your next life.

Hey, at least we're all human, right?

## MORALITY SCORE

**Marriages: three. Alleged affairs: two. Naughty teachers: one.**

# Ann Coulter

**Media Pundit**

"I will go to a black church and talk about gay marriage. The brothers aren't big on queer theory."

*—in the* New York Observer, *2002*

"Oh, I think they'll burn in hell."

*—in response to a question regarding gays in an interview with the* Telegraph *(London), 2002*

## Her Remarkable Career

T he quotes above are just two examples of conservative media pundit Ann Coulter's razor-sharp, knee-slapping wit. A regular Voltaire, Coulter is the author of three *New York Times* bestsellers, *Slander, Treason,* and *High Crimes and Misdemeanors* (titles that are hilariously self-referential), as well as *How to Talk to a Liberal (If You Must)*. With her long blond locks and spindly frame, Coulter has the frothing look of a dog about to be put down.

Drawn by her charm and religious conviction ("God gave us the earth. We have dominion over the plants, the animals, the trees. God said, 'Earth is yours. Take it. Rape it. It's yours.'"), talk-show producers and radio hosts have kept Coulter booked and her face and voice omnipresent.

But before she was a shrill, screeching hack peddling nature-rape fantasies (and, doubtless, countless Ann Coulter fantasies) to ham-fisted rednecks, Coulter was a smart chick, albeit a flaming conservative smart chick. Raised in New Canaan, Connecticut, Coulter attended Cornell University, moving on to the University of Michigan for a law degree, where she founded the local chapter of the Federalist Society and edited the *Michigan Law Review*. Later, she spent time in the Justice Department, working as an attorney, and later became an appeals court clerk before moving into corporate law in Manhattan.

When the Republican coup took place in Congress in 1994, Coulter moved to D.C. to work for Senator Spencer Abraham (R-Michigan), who was to the Federalist Society the equivalent of a *Sports Illustrated* swimsuit model.

Eventually, though, in the progressive tradition of empowered women everywhere, Coulter realized her looks could get her places her education couldn't. (As for that hack Gloria Steinem, according to Coulter, she had to sleep with a liberal in order to get her magazine off the ground.) Actually, wait—no, it was God who told her to flaunt her stuff on television. As Coulter told the *St. Petersburg Times:* "God just decided, we've got enough lawyers; you are supposed to be on TV."

By mid-1996, Coulter was beginning to saturate the market, appearing on MSNBC, CNN, ABC, and writing for the *National Review,* as well as her own syndicated column.

Her inane and tedious drivel, described by her Republican flunkies as "candor," drew attention. As former ambassador Pamela Harriman's casket was being carried off a plane, Coulter, the epitome of conservative class, described Harriman as a woman who had slept her way to the top. MSNBC put Coulter on probation for this comment, but fired her for the next: telling a disabled Vietnam vet that "people like you caused us to lose that war." She and the *National Review* parted company after Coulter submitted a column suggesting a solution to the Muslim "problem": "We should invade their countries, kill their leaders, and convert them to Christianity."

## Her Personal Commitment

Despite being one of the most overcompensating members of the Protect Marriage Fan Club, Coulter herself has never been married, which makes her an expert on such matters. Her expertise is enhanced by her rich dating history. There was that Democratic Senate staffer whose policies she opposes. Then James Tully. Dinesh D'Souza. Bill Maher. Then that FBI agent. Totally innocent fun. In fact, Coulter has been engaged four times.

But then there was Bob Guccione, Jr. Despite claims to be supportive of the antipornography movement, Coulter dated the son of Bob Guccione. Not just another Italian in black leather, Bob Guccione is the publisher of *Penthouse*. His son, Bob Guccione, Jr., was referred to affectionately by his girl-friend as "The Gooch."

Perhaps it was the influence of "The Gooch," but Coulter, that hard-line conservative, told Geraldo Rivera in 2000 that it was perfectly okay to sleep around: "Let's say I go out every night, I meet a guy and have sex with him. Good for me. I'm not married." But then God came knocking to remind her that, along with homosexuality, sleeping around before marriage is a no-no, so she told the London *Telegraph*:

"I will never say publicly that, as a Christian, I think God says it's okay to have premarital sex or to have homosexual sex." Oops. Well, you already did, Ann.

Of course, like every other self-appointed pontiff profiled in this book, Coulter's arbitrary social rules apply only to others. Stumbling along the talk-show circuit like a badly drawn political cartoon, she seems completely unaware of her own irony.

"Women like Pamela Harriman and Patricia Duff are basically Anna Nicole Smith from the waist down," Coulter told *Salon* in 2000. "Let's just call it for what it is. They're whores."

The criticism of Anna Nicole Smith is particularly cutting. Using one's sexuality to grab public attention despite nonsensical blabber? Blond hair? Short skirts? How scandalous.

---

### MORALITY SCORE

Marriages: zero. Engagements: four. Ironic attacks on other blondes who use their looks to get ahead: countless. Assertions that gays will burn in hell: (at least) one. Porn industry boyfriends: one.

# Gary Bauer

**Failed Presidential Candidate
and Compassionate Conservative**

The words "husband" and "wife" will be meaningless. Homosexual adoption will be instantly legalized and generations of children will be raised in wholly unnatural environments—deprived of ever having the benefit of a mother and a father. The public schools will teach your children that two men "marrying" each other are morally equivalent to one man and one woman. It's legal, so it must be okay! Our kids will be taught how to perform "safe sodomy" in their sex education classes.

—*Gary Bauer, "Why We Must Defend
Marriage Now," 2004*

## His Remarkable Career

**B**auer has been beating it for most of his career. The Bible, that is. After dodging the Vietnam draft, like so many of our upstanding legislators (in the form of a deferment), this janitor's son from Kentucky went into civil service. In the eighties, the Reagan White House was the place for hot, young radical conservatives to be, and Bauer was all up in that. He served in the Reagan administration for eight years, including two as a senior domestic policy advisor. Bauer was named chairman of Reagan's Special Working Group on the Family, where he produced a report called "The Family: Preserving America's Future." Bauer rocked the party line like an Ecstasy-addled goth kid, claiming the National Endowment for the Arts was run by "a small cadre of cultural revolutionaries, militant homosexuals, and anti-religious bigots who are intent on attacking the average American's most deeply held beliefs while sending them the bill."

Bauer's break into the big business of fear and (self-) loathing came when Dr. James Dobson brought him on board the Family Research Council, a squawking, über-conservative organization that devalues non-Christians, non-heteros, and nonfamilies. Dobson, a seasoned hater, hired Bauer to lead the innocuous-sounding Family Research Council, and Bauer spent a decade expanding the nonprofit from three staffers and a $1 million a year budget to a payroll of 120 employees and a budget of $14 million per year.

FRC is an organization that is full of proponents of the gays-can-be-turned-straight program. "The Family Research Council applauds the efforts of men and women who provide counseling and support for people who wish to leave

homosexuality and find fulfillment in a healthy lifestyle."
When challenged by a gay student about this recipe for
unhappy marriages, Bauer said: "I can't think of a greater
oppression than to try to force somebody to continue to live
as apparently you and some others here are living."

Unless you're Gary Bauer trying to force somebody to
live as "apparently" he and some others (in this book) are living. No. Then it's called being a "loving Christian."

In 2000, Bauer decided to holy roll for president. He ran on
a platform of "family values": this included a rabid antiabortion policy, stances on homosexuality that could politely
be termed "antigay," and the kind of religious agenda that
deems bogus all non-Christian religions.

He lost the election.

## His Personal Commitment

Adultery is a big deal," Bauer once commented. "Harry
Truman knew this: 'How can I trust a man if his wife
cannot?' the plainspoken man from Independence said."

Truman. An interesting role model for a guy whose wife
can't trust him.

The turnover rate among Gary Bauer's campaign staff is
almost as bad as Wal-Mart's: nine of his senior staffers quit
in protest, not over the politician's policies, but over the long
hours Bauer spent behind closed doors with his hot twenty-

six-year-old deputy campaign manager, Melissa McClard.
Even Bauer's loyal secretary for fifteen years left in disgust.

Being good radical conservatives, Bauer's irked staffers
never put into words what they thought the boss was doing
with McClard, but the phrase "You shall know them by their
fruits" rings a bell. The farthest out on the limb any of them
would go was to say publicly that they believed Bauer had
engaged in "inappropriate behavior" with the twenty-six-
year-old.

The rumors forced Bauer to call a press conference,
where he categorically denied having an affair with McClard
and brought along his wife and three children as humiliated
supporters. He patiently explained that he met with *all* his
staff members . . . in private . . . for hours at a time . . . except
for those staffers who quit in protest of those meetings they
were never invited to that took place in private for hours at
a time.

"These rumors and character assassination are disgusting, outrageous, evil, and sick," Bauer said. "They are trash-
can politics at its worst. . . . I have not violated my vows."
But he also said that, as a regular old Joe, he should not be
held to such strict standards of Christian morality: "I am not
a minister . . . I am not a pastor."

But the press conference backfired. Instead of clearing his
name, Bauer pissed off preachers and his bosses at the Family Research Council. Dr. Dobson gave Bauer a stern warning
from the Big Guy, and repositioned Bauer's holy tinfoil hat to

better block out the idea of spending hours in private quarters with cute staffers.

Now, let's flash back to April 13, 1998, when Gary Bauer faced a group of Harvard University students at the Kennedy School of Government, who grilled him about his stance on homosexuality. In response to one question, he said: "When you come into the public square and suggest that the rest of America needs to redefine marriage as between two men and two women, or when you come into the public square and insist on the right in the public schools in America to teach my children that the way you have chosen is no morally different from the way I have chosen to live with my wife, you should, in a rational, reasonable world, expect opposition."

Bauer followed the shining path to become a Bush minion in the 2004 presidential campaign. As president of the 527 group Americans United to Preserve Marriage, he funded a $500,000 television ad campaign in Michigan and Pennsylvania titled "Kerry Too Liberal for America."

In his latest position as president of an organization called American Values, whose motto reads "Your Voice to Help Protect Life, Marriage, Family, Faith, and Freedom," Bauer claims to be a loving Christian. If only Christ knew.

In reality, Bauer's loving kindness comes in the form of hate speech—accusing gays of being disease-ridden sodomites, and lobbying on the Hill to have anti–hate crime laws repealed. And he appeals to those ever-thrifty conservatives by telling them that, if gays are allowed to marry, conservatives' pocketbooks will take a hit. "Homosexual 'spouses' will suddenly be entitled to health insurance benefits and, given the high rates of disease and other medical issues associated with the lifestyle, all of us will pay even more for health insurance."

---

### MORALITY SCORE

**Wives: one. Kids: three. Hours behind closed doors with a hot, blond twenty-six-year-old: countless. Dollars of soft money diverted to radical conservative antigay causes: millions.**

# Alan Keyes

**Luckless Politician**

The essence of . . . family life remains procreation. If we embrace homosexuality as a
proper basis for marriage, we are saying that
it's possible to have a marriage state that in
principle excludes procreation and is based
simply on the premise of selfish hedonism.

—*former Republican Senate candidate Alan Keyes*

## His Remarkable Career

If there were a lifetime achievement award for political
mediocrity, Alan Keyes—or, the Man Who Would Be
Obama—would finally be a viable candidate for something.
Everything seemed to be in place for political success: Keyes
earned a PhD in government from Harvard. He spent eleven
years with the U.S. State Department. He served in the U.S.
Foreign Service. He was a member of the National Security
Council before becoming ambassador, under Ronald Reagan, to the U.N. Economic and Social Council.

So far, so good, right? A little right-leaning, but no great
shakes. But then, like Pinky from *Pinky and the Brain*, Keyes
began his quest to "take over the world."

It began innocently enough. He founded National Tax-payers' Action Day. Then he was "nominated" for the U.S. Senate in Maryland (an achievement touted in his official biography—but he won the primary, not the Senate seat). With this track record of electoral success, Keyes took the natural next step and declared himself a presidential candidate in 1996 and 2000.

The Keyes platform was unabashedly conservative. By, in his words, "eloquently elevating" the national political debate, Keyes took his pro-life and "pro-family" views to the podium in the primary debates.

But the real highlight of Keyes's career came in his 2004 bid for the Illinois Senate. He was by then well established as the Republican go-to guy for failed high-profile campaigns. Once Republican candidate Jack Ryan dropped from the race on the heels of his seedy sex scandal, the good old boys imported Keyes from Maryland.

His misguided run was doomed from the start when TV stations across the country began replaying an old clip of Keyes griping about Hillary Clinton running for senate in a state where she didn't even live: New York. But, like so many Republicans before him, Keyes was completely undeterred by his own bald-faced hypocrisy. If nothing else, he was emboldened, his logic sharpened. At a Marquette Park rally against same-sex marriage, he told the crowd, "If we do not know who the mother is, who the father is, without knowing all the brothers and sisters, incest becomes inevitable."

## His Personal Commitment

There's one thing Alan Keyes wants you to know about him; it's that he is a "dedicated family man" whose "stated purpose in life, like that of America's founders, is to provide a secure future for our posterity."

But after his daughter, Maya Marcel-Keyes, publicly announced that she was gay, Keyes helped secure her posterity by disowning her, tossing her out of the house, and refusing to pay her college tuition. Maybe for this Harvard man it was that Ivy League rivalry: Maya had been accepted to Brown.

Maya had always worked hard on her father's campaigns, even though she disagreed with "almost everything" on his platform. During his campaign against Barack Obama for that Illinois Senate seat, Keyes publicly called Dick Cheney's daughter Mary, who is an open lesbian, a "selfish hedonist" and—the double whammy—"a sinner." In the same interview, completely unsolicited, Keyes offered this: "If my daughter were a lesbian, I'd look at her and say, 'That is a relationship that is based on selfish hedonism.' I would also tell my daughter that it's a sin and she needs to pray to the Lord God to help her deal with that sin." Maya was listening to those comments.

"It was kind of strange that he said it like a hypothetical. It was really kind of unpleasant," Maya said. Maya has said in interviews that her parents had known of their daughter's sexual orientation since just before she graduated high school.

Keyes—that dedicated family man—stopped speaking to his daughter and threw her out of the house. In 2005, a well-organized group of selfish hedonists, the Point Foundation (a gay charity that provides college funds to students who have faced difficulties because of their sexual orientation) decided to cover Maya's college expenses.

MORALITY SCORE

**Professions of a singular dedication to family values: numerous.
Dismissed lesbian daughters: one.**

# Rush Limbaugh

**Conservative Talk-Show Host and Ex–Drug Addict**

> There's something deeply troubling about undercutting marriage and undercutting the Boy Scouts in order to get to some notion of equal rights. There's something just doesn't follow there. In order to get to equal rights, we've got to undercut marriage and we've got to undercut the Boy Scouts and who knows what else. And, by the way, if an institution works as it is, we've got to weaken it, we've got to undercut it in the name of equal rights.
>
> *—Rush Limbaugh on why he supports*
> *a ban on same-sex marriage*

## His Remarkable Career

Often called a right-wing Howard Stern, Rush Limbaugh has a talk show that airs on more than six hundred radio stations, and can boast twenty million "Dittohead" listeners. Though both Limbaugh and Stern are blowhards, only one is a former drug addict. And it's not the one with long hair. It's the one who claims that he is "talent on loan from God."

Born in Cape Girardeau, Missouri, in 1951, our man Rush was a radioman from the start. A boil on his butt might've literally saved his ass, when his pilonidal cyst (a chronic draining sinus located in the opening between the buttocks) got him out of military service during Vietnam. Rush then cruised from radio station to radio station until he found one that gave him his career high. But, as sometimes happens to cruisers, he was rejected by two radio stations, both of which fired him. He spent some time working for the Kansas City Royals, but found his way back into radio. In the 1980s, he was hired to host a radio program in San Diego, taking over Morton Downey Jr.'s old time slot, which was a zygote of his wildly popular show, which peaked during the Clinton administration. Drawing fans with his wit and charm ("Feminism was established to allow unattractive women easier access to the mainstream"—which begs the question, was conservative talk radio established to allow unattractive men easier access to the mainstream?), Rush became the darling of the long-suffering conservative diaspora. In 1988, Rush made the move to Manhattan, where he hit the big time with his talk show. You know, the one that conservatives claim helped them stage the 1994 Republican coup? Today, his syndicated spew reaches across AM radio stations from coast to coast. He not only "reshaped" political talk radio, he made AM channels sound shriller than ever.

On his show, Rush was pro-war, pro-marriage, antidrug, and antigay. In his life, his scorecard looked like this: three marriages, three divorces, one confessed drug habit, and a federal investigation into his alleged "doctor shopping" for the pain pills he was addicted to.

## His Personal Commitment

Like Bob Barr, Rush Limbaugh has found that the sacred institution of marriage has no three-strikes-and-you're-out rule. In 1977, he married a radio station secretary named Roxy Maxine McNeely. The marriage lasted three years. In 1983 he married a Kansas City Royal Stadium usher named Michelle Sixta. The union lasted five years. In between his second and third marriages, Rush began dispensing marital advice to his listeners, saying: "If you want a successful marriage, let your husband do what he wants to do."

With a blank check like that, how could any marriage be more stable?

One day, a college student at the University of North Florida e-mailed Rush, asking how she should go about standing up to her anti-Reagan professor. Rush never wrote back. After hearing Rush discuss a letter he received from some flight attendants, the scorned college student, Marta Fitzgerald, wrote a searing letter to Rush. This time, he responded. In short order, the two were married—at Clarence Thomas's Virginia home. Also in attendance was that proponent of family values William Bennett—who would later admit to a multimillion-dollar gambling habit. With Thomas and Bennett as witnesses, Rush's third marriage was off to an auspicious start. (Note: it was really quite open-minded of Rush to have Thomas officiate at his wedding, especially since it was not so long ago that he'd said: "Why should blacks be heard? They're twelve percent of the population. Who the hell cares?")

In 2003, the shit hit the fan when the *National Enquirer* revealed that Rush was addicted to painkillers. His drug of choice was Vicodin (hydrocodone), in the same family as heroin. Interestingly enough, this story was true—and Rush, in October of 2003, admitted in court that he was, indeed, hooked on illegal drugs. Those of his listeners who might have been confused by this turn of events needed only to reflect upon Rush's comments about what to do with these kinds of people:

> Drug use, some might say, is destroying this country. And we have laws against selling drugs, pushing drugs, using drugs, importing drugs. And so if people are violating the law by doing drugs, they ought to be accused and they ought to be convicted and they ought to be sent up.

Come on, let's be serious: drug addicts who marry their third wives in the living room of a disgraced Supreme Court justice don't get "sent up"—they go back on the air a month later, just in time to jump into the same-sex-marriage debate.

As the debate was raging in Massachusetts in 2004, Rush took what seemed to be the safe route of reasoning: "Marriage is about raising children. That's the purpose of the institution." An interesting line of reasoning from a man who, despite three marriages, has no children of his own.

And the chances of a little Rush are diminishing. In June 2004, Rush announced that he and Marta were splitting up for undisclosed reasons. The world is currently holding its collective breath to see how much of this fiscally conservative but morally upstanding recovering addict's money will go to the coed he met online.

---

**MORALITY SCORE**

**Marriages: three. Divorces: three.
Children: zero. Ass boils: one.**

# Representative Dick Armey

## (R·TEXAS)

Yes, I am Dick Armey. And if there is a "dick army," Barney Frank would want to join up.
>—*Dick Armey, referring to openly gay congressman Barney Frank*

## His Remarkable Career

The enlightened voters of the Twenty-sixth District of Texas sent Richard Keith Armey to the House of Representatives in 1984. The former economics professor, and professional lech, went on to coauthor the Contract with America, along with moral paragon Newt Gingrich. Later, he'd go on to vote for the Defense of Marriage Act, though too late to defend one of his own from himself. Like many of his contemporary ideological gasbags, Armey threw fits over Bill Clinton's sexual escapades, even though he himself was an old pervert who enjoyed getting up close and personal with his female students back in the days when he was a professor at North Texas University (now the University of North Texas).

"If it were me that had documented personal conduct along the lines of the president's," Armey blustered at the time of impeachment, "I would be so filled with shame that I would resign."

Like many good congressional Christians, Armey never skipped a chance to approve another war, even though he never served a day in his life. Though he was cleverly disguised as a "pro-defense" Republican, Armey created a so-called Nonpolitical Commission that shut down military bases. Armey was eventually elevated to House majority leader, second only to fellow man-ho' Newt Gingrich, where he voted to ban gay adoptions in Washington, D.C.

As a Presbyterian and a blowhard who spouted off things like "values agendas" that applied to anybody's life but his own, Armey was beloved by groups of religious, antigay automatons like the Family Research Council. "Dick Armey is someone who has worked very closely with conservatives all these years," the vice president of government relations at the FRC told Citizen Link. "He has done the Lord's work."

Apparently, the Lord likes playing grab-ass with coeds. And he likes divorce, too.

## His Personal Commitment

In 1998, Trent Lott made his infamously tolerant statements about homosexuality: it was not only a sin, but it was a *disease* akin to kleptomania. In the aftermath, Dick

Armey rushed to the senator's defense. He literally pulled out his heavily thumbed through Bible and said: "The Bible is very clear on this. Both myself and Senator Lott believe very strongly in the Bible." And then: "I abide by the instructions that are given me in the Bible."

Reeeaaaaaalllly, Representative Armey. Aren't you a guy who divorced his wife and married a student in one of his economics classes? Well, let's check that out. And hey, we'll even use your source (italics added).

> . . . the Lord witnessed the vows you and your wife made to each other on your wedding day when you were young. But you have been disloyal to her, though she remained your faithful companion, the wife of your marriage vows. Didn't the Lord make you one with your wife? In body and spirit you are his. And what does he want? Godly children from your union. So guard yourself; remain loyal to the wife of your youth. *"For I hate divorce!" says the Lord, the God of Israel.* "It is as cruel as putting on a victim's bloodstained coat," says the Lord Almighty. "So guard yourself; always remain loyal to your wife."
>
> —*Malachi 2: 14–16*

Think the Old Testament is totally passé, outdated, and irrelevent? You a New Testament kind of believer? Well, Armey's screwed from both sides of the BC/AD divide:

> Jesus replied, "Moses permitted divorce as a concession to your hard-hearted wickedness, but it was not what God had originally intended. And I tell you this, a man who divorces his wife and marries another commits adultery—unless his wife has been unfaithful."
>
> —*Matthew 19: 8–9*

Oh, and: "Jesus told them, *"Whoever divorces his wife and marries someone else commits adultery against her"* (Mark 10: 11–12).

In a remarkably rare demonstration of ideological consistency, Armey was never documented trying to have sex with men. His female econ students were a different story. Three years before he said publicly that he would resign if he had "documented conduct" like Clinton's, Armey's sleazy conduct had already been documented. In May 1995, the *Dallas Observer* revealed that Armey had persistently tried to trickle a little lovin' down his female economics students' supply sides while teaching at North Texas University.

Three students publicly claimed that Armey had sexually harassed them. And should you mistakenly think these were just more Paula Joneses, think again: Susan Aileen White earned a master's degree in economics from North Texas, Anna Weniger later became New Mexico's state economist, and Anne Marie Best became a professor of economics at Lamar University. One of these students, Weniger, was upset enough about the alleged harassment to quit the college entirely. At least one of his students didn't mind an Armey of Dick: his current and second wife, Susan.

Then there was that whole kerfuffle with Massachusetts Congressman Barney Frank, an openly gay Democrat. Referring to the estimable congressman as "Barney Fag," Armey used the convincing excuse that he had "trouble with alliteration."

Armey retired from the House in 2003 and now enjoys such congressional retirement pastimes as bass fishing and lobbying at Piper Rudnick in Washington, D.C. His most recent book, *Armey's Axioms,* wisely omits degrading jokes about his own unfortunate moniker.

## MORALITY SCORE

**Marriages: two. Divorces: one. Public claims of sexual harassment: three. Votes to ban gay adoptions: one. Hypocritical defenses of homophobic comments by citing biblical passages: one. Alliterative accidents: one.**

# Laura Schlessinger, PhD (in Physiology)

## Radio Talk-Show Host

> Political activists have successfully reposi-
> tioned sexual deviancy as a constitutionally
> protected "lifestyle" equivalent in every way to
> heterosexuality. . . . This is not about discrimi-
> nation against homosexuals.
>
> —*Laura Schlessinger,* Parenthood by Proxy

## Her Remarkable Career

The female Limbaugh of the frontal lobe, Laura
Schlessinger—known to her fans as "Dr. Laura"—is
the host of a popular radio talk show that reaches nearly
twenty million listeners who are aghast at the good doctor's
edgy maxims, like "Stop whining!"

Seeking pat answers to lifelong problems and moral
dilemmas, Schlessinger's fans subject themselves to the cat-
o'-nine-tails, a torture device that is studded with sound

bites. Dr. Laura is not an MD, she is a PhD—of physiology, not psychology or psychiatry. The California Board of Behavioral Science decrees that "nobody is allowed to use 'Doctor' unless they are a medical doctor or . . . a professor in the psychological field with a clinical license." But now we're just being petty.

Schlessinger is a licensed counselor, but widely referred to as a psychoanalyst. She does little to correct false perceptions of her credentials. And her "recommendations" come with the homophobe's seal of approval: along with strictures such as no premarital sex and no marriage before thirty, Schlessinger has long maintained—and quite vociferously—that homosexuality is a biological error that must be corrected.

Like Limbaugh, Dr. Laura rode the waves of popular sentiment in the nineties as Republicans became more and more disenchanted with Clinton's complete failure to tank the economy. They started buying her books with titles like *How Could You Do That?* and *Ten Stupid Things Women Do to Mess Up Their Lives.* When her hypnotized minions turned their ire toward gays, the doctor pleaded for tolerance, saying that gays were not evil—they were simply victims, biological errors. And they could be saved, even if homosexuality was, as the doctor put it herself, akin to murder.

"When we have the word 'homosexual,' we are clarifying the dysfunction, the deviancy, the reality. We change it to the word 'gay,' it makes it more difficult to pinpoint the truth. So one of the things that the homosexual agenda did was to change the name. Just like somebody complained to me yesterday about ethnic cleansing, that it sounds like washing machine as opposed to murder. They were right. Ethnic cleansing sounds nice. Murder is the truth, homosexuality is the truth. Gay isn't."

Deviancy. It's one of Dr. Laura's favorite words. Because she preaches that healthy regimen of no sex before thirty, she leans on the word "deviant" to describe any departure from the path.

It doesn't take someone with a doctorate in, uh, physiology to understand the concept of projection. Let's peek inside the unauthorized biography of Dr. Laura Schlessinger to see what all the projection is about.

"I pretty much preach, teach, and nag," Schlessinger once told the *Washington Post*. "It's not pop psychology at all. If anything, it's a new genre." For now, let's call that genre *Hypocrisy for Dummies*.

## Her Personal Commitment

Dr. Laura got in bed with fame in 1975. When she was in her late twenties, the married Schlessinger called in to a popular women's issues radio show, hosted by a guy named Bill Ballance. The pressing women's issue on the table that day? Widow or divorcée—which would you rather be? Like boxers or briefs, the side you chose presumably would reveal much about your character. Schlessinger wanted to be a widow.

Ballance kept the young future shrew on the air for twenty minutes, then agreed, off air, to meet her. He later made her a regular guest on the show. Together, Ballance and Schlessinger developed the call-and-confess radio talk-show formula, a format that allowed the shrill to be shriller and the confessors to be publicly reprimanded. It was a formula that was, of course, later cloned by hundreds of radio and TV shows across the country. And it wasn't long before the would-be widow had her own show, the eponymous *Dr. Laura.*

But lest you think Laura Schlessinger was all work, no play—or a thirty-year-old virgin—consider her hobbies at that time. Amateur photography. Like many conservative moralists, Dr. Laura didn't live up to her own dogma. Although she was married before the age of thirty (shame on you, Laura!), there's no telling if she engaged in premarital sex. Instead, she opted for extramarital sex. After becoming a regular on Ballance's show, Schlessinger became a regular in his bed.

Her husband—the first one—did not do Schlessinger the service of making her a widow. Instead, he made her a divorcée. And while Schlessinger worked her ass off for Ballance—who was thirty years her senior and a real looker, with his TV anchor pompadour and tinted glasses—she also helped him out with some snapshots.

In 1975, Ballance snapped some photographs of a very willing Dr. Laura in various states of undress. Twenty-three years later, while she was at the peak of her career, Ballance screwed her one last time—selling a dozen nude photos of her to Internet Entertainment Group (most famous for the Tommy and Pam sex tape) for a reported $50,000.

After Dr. Laura sued IEG and lost, the company posted the photographs on their Web site free for one week, waiving a $24.95 membership fee so users could feast their eyes on a radio morality diva, photographed by her boss spread-eagled and giggling like a pin-up girl.

The deviance was so thick, you could cut it with a knife.

While she stopped short of calling herself a biological error, Dr. Laura blamed the photographs and the adulterous affair on a brief dalliance—not with Ballance but with atheism.

"I've undergone profound changes over the course of my life from atheist to observant Jew," she said. "I am mystified as to why this eighty-year-old man would do such a morally reprehensible thing."

Although her career wasn't exactly ruined by the morally reprehensible act of producing proof of hypocrisy, Dr. Laura's profile was definitely lowered as the nineties came to a close. Ever self-righteous, Schlessinger continues her radio show, writes books, and spews the same hateful antigay rhetoric. And while she might have looked good on film when she was in her twenties, her television viewers decided she had a face for radio as she reached her fifties, and her short-lived TV show was axed.

## MORALITY SCORE

Rabid right-wing radio shows: one. Condemnation of gays for being biological errors: countless. Confirmed adulterous affairs: one. Naked photos taken while engaged in a confirmed adulterous affair: twelve. Times atheism took the heat for a moral failure: one.

# Representative Henry Hyde

## (R·ILLINOIS, RETIRED)

> It demeans, it lowers the concept of marriage by making it something that it should not be and is not, celebrating conduct that is not approved by the majority of the people.
> —*Henry Hyde on homosexuality, addressing Congress on July 12, 1996*

## His Remarkable Career

For decades, Representative Henry Hyde was one of the most respected, and right-wing, members of Congress. A Roman Catholic (you know, those folks who consider marriage sacred and adultery a mortal sin), Hyde supported the Defense of Marriage Act and the Federal Marriage Amendment (you know, those bills that make marriage sacred and emphasize that adultery is a sin). Perhaps most famously, though, Representative Henry Hyde led the charge for impeachment proceedings against President Bill Clinton in 1998, stemming from Papa Clinton's relationship with

Monica Lewinsky. As chair of the House Judiciary Committee, Hyde moved to impeach Clinton for, as he was always very careful to emphasize, his "public acts" of lying under oath, not for any of that blue-dress-staining activity that took place privately. Why so careful, Hank? Well, maybe because he was already a member of the club.

## His Personal Commitment

In 1998, as Hyde, Newt Gingrich, and company strung up their presidential piñata, *Salon* published an article about a seventy-six-year-old man who was living in a subsidized apartment in Weston, Florida. In the article, titled "This Hypocrite Broke Up My Family," Fred Snodgrass, the ex-husband of one Cherie Snodgrass, claimed that seeing Hyde on television prattling on about morality was turning his stomach. The remedy for upset stomach? Coming forward and revealing that thirty years earlier, Hyde had played Hide Little Hank with Snodgrass's then wife and mother of his three children—all while Hyde himself was married and raising four boys.

"These politicians were going on about how [Hyde] should have been on the Supreme Court, what a great man he is, how we're lucky to have him in Congress in charge of the impeachment case," Snodgrass told *Salon*. "And all I can think of is here is this man, this hypocrite who broke up my family."

Five years of extramarital bliss, all while keeping Cherie penned up like a harem girl in a lush downtown apartment, managed to desanctify both Snodgrass's marriage and Hyde's. One day, when Fred decided to confront his wife at her Hyde-funded bachelorette pad, Hyde was already there. WWJD? Jesus would, apparently, bar the door while Cherie buttoned up her blouse.

Frustrated, Fred finally confronted Hyde's wife, and the affair ended. Cherie came crawling back to Fred, who agreed to take her back. But the sanctity of the Snodgrass marriage had taken too large a hit from heavy hitter Hank Hyde, and it ended.

Before departing for good, Cherie Snodgrass did leave her husband with two mementos of their marriage: a picture of her sitting on Hyde's lap in a Chicago nightclub, and photo of Hyde himself, signed "I love you, Cherie!!!! Hank, Dec. 30, 1966!"

Before publishing the story, *Salon*'s editorial staff had the tiniest inkling that the Republican leadership might blame the White House for the publication of this story, so they ran an accompanying editorial that explained how they got the story in the first place: Snodgrass's friend, seeing his friend's stomach so upset, called *Salon*. *Salon* called Snodgrass. Story runs.

But all this detailed explanation led House Majority Whip Tom DeLay (R-Texas) to one conclusion. Bill Clinton did it! The whip asked the FBI to open an investigation, hoping for charges of extortion against the president (extorting congressmen, presumably, to vote nay on the impeachment charge or else have their own adulterous affairs revealed).

For his part, Hyde dismissed the affair as a "youthful indiscretion" and advised *Salon* that the "statute of limitations" on such activities had long since expired. However, after mounting pressure, he tendered his resignation from the chairmanship of the House Judiciary Committee. Speaker Gingrich rejected it. Looking back, Gingrich probably didn't want to set a precedent of axing people over recently unearthed sex scandals. But that's another story.

What happened to our hero? Well, as punishment for being the long-suffering husband of Hyde's mistress, Fred Snodgrass wound up living three thousand miles away from his ex-wife and three estranged children in a government-subsidized apartment—known in the real estate industry as a "shit hole." Hanky Panky spent his life winning popularity contests, impeaching presidents for their moral shortcomings and their defilement of the institution of marriage, and testifying as a character witness for men like Joseph Scheidler, whom a federal jury found guilty of 120 counts of criminal predicate acts of violence in connection with shutting down abortion clinics. (Hyde also compared abortion clinics to Auschwitz.)

## MORALITY SCORE

**Ruined husbands: one. Fatherless children: three. Slighted mistresses: one. Impeached president: one. Unforgivable metaphors: one.**

# Senator Phil Gramm

## (R·TEXAS, RETIRED)

A great peril.

*—Phil Gramm, describing same-sex
marriage during the run up to the
Defense of Marriage Act, 1996*

## His Remarkable Career

Former Republican senator and would-be pornographer Phil Gramm was a leading culture warrior-clown of the family values era. While he opposed legislation that would make it easier to end life inside the womb, he favored legislation that made it easier to end life outside the womb: deregulating weapons and nuclear bombs. He voted to terminate affirmative action. He voted to end special funding for businesses owned by women and minorities. He voted against expanding the definition of hate crimes to include sexual orientation. He voted against prohibiting job discrimination based on sexual orientation. He voted yes on expanding the federal government's wiretap privileges on cell phones.

Gramm is a man with his priorities in order.

While he may be all about the guns and nurse hawkish sentiments, Gramm (keeping in step with so many of our brave politicians) never served. Instead, he applied for five deferments during the Vietnam war. After graduating from Georgia Military Academy, he chose a career as an economics professor at Texas A&M University. A Republican from Texas who taught economics at a university, and is hiding a shady moral background rife with hypocrisy and a penchant for regressive social policy? It's downright shocking (or the result of too much inbreeding).

In 1978, Gramm mustered the gumption to take his guff to the capital—as a Democrat. In 1983, he swapped sides and won a special election to keep his seat, as a Republican. In 1984, Gramm took advantage of some polling data he came across that indicated that homosexuality could be used as a successful wedge issue in a campaign. Gramm wedged away, courting what Gramm himself called "the redneck vote." The rednecks loved him and hated gays, and so Gramm remained an elected official. As the years passed, Gramm grew more and more reactionary, until he became known as one of the Republicans on the farthest end of the right-wing spectrum. By his second term, he was chairing the Senate Committee on Banking, Housing and Urban Affairs. Like his pro-marriage and pro-military stances, his take on small government was likewise fabricated. Gramm bragged of his slick deals to help his home state on the taxpayer dime with his famous saying, "I'm carrying so much pork, I'm beginning to get trichinosis."

Of course, it's a bad grocer who gives his pork away. One fellow who purchased a plate of Gramm's down-home jowl bacon was the convicted savings-and-loan swindler Jerry D. Stiles. Stiles fronted Gramm $117,000, interest free. Gramm used the cash to bring a Texas contractor to Maryland and build himself a vacation home. Gramm paid back just $60,000 and Stiles covered the difference out of his own pocket. Who knew that bankers were that generous?*

Though he deserved at least a few censures of his own, Gramm vehemently opposed censuring Bill Clinton. This wasn't Christian compassion. Instead, Gramm wanted desperately to impeach the philandering Philistine. Crimes should not go unpunished.

Yet, according to *Mother Jones,* Gramm had once been a compassionate conservative: in 1979, Gramm repeatedly lobbied for the parole of convicted drug and weapons dealer Bill Doyle. When Gramm's letters arrived, the prison gates flew open, and Doyle roamed free. Until he was arrested and charged with more drug charges. Oh, did we mention that Gramm called Bill Clinton "soft" on drug dealers and criticized Michael Dukakis for releasing Willie Horton?

---

*Coincidentally, Gramm then greased the wheels to pass a law for ailing (read: mismanaged) S&Ls to stay open. He also urged federal regulators to give Stiles waivers even as they investigated Stiles. The Senate ruled that the shady $57,000 payout wasn't a bribe but a "cost overrun."

In his later years, he started on the sanctity of marriage tract. A sweetheart of the Christian Coalition, Gramm vehemently opposed legalizing same-sex unions and used as his rationale the importance of protecting the sacred union between a man and a woman that serves as the foundation for our society. Along with Alan Keyes, Gramm attended a rally sponsored by the Coalition and other right-wing groups and signed a document called "The Marriage Protection Resolution." The resolution read, in part:

> Whereas marriage is an essential element in the foundation of a healthy society, and whereas government has a duty to protect the foundation, resolved, the state should not legitimize homosexual relationships by legalizing same-sex "marriage" but should continue to reserve the special sanction of civil marriage for one man and one woman, husband and wife.

## His Personal Commitment

This guard dog of the "special sanction" and family values omits the details of his own first union. Most people don't know Gramm is on his second marriage. The divorce doesn't stop Gramm from positioning himself as a moral paragon who publicly frets over the devaluation of

American virtues, and votes to deny marriage to those who would, quite possibly, be more successful at it than him. If gays can't marry, why would it be so outlandish to outlaw interracial marriages again? Surprisingly, Gramm isn't really pushing this one. Perhaps that's because his second wife, former Enron director Wendy Gramm, is a Korean woman.

Add to divorce, that violation of biblical law, the fact that Gramm tried to make a skin flick. George Caton, Gramm's brother-in-law, said that in 1974 he watched a film called *Truck Stop Women* with Gramm. This Oscar-worthy movie gave the economics professor an idea for a real moneymaker: a raunchy film called *Beauty Queens*. Gramm later admitted that he sank $7,500 of his own money into the movie, though he denies that it was a porno. The movie's producers actually hoodwinked Gramm and used the cash to make an unknown spoof about Richard Nixon.

## MORALITY SCORE

**Christian Coalition–sponsored anti–same sex marriage resolutions signed: one. Votes against ending discrimination and hate crimes based on sexual orientation: three. Divorces: one.**

# Representative
# Helen Chenoweth

## (R-IDAHO, RETIRED)

Our Founding Fathers knew that political leaders' personal conduct must be held to the highest standards. President Clinton's behavior has severely damaged his ability to lead our nation and the free world. To restore honor to public office, and the trust of the American people, we must affirm that personal conduct does count, and integrity matters.

—*Helen Chenoweth in a 1998 campaign advertisement*

## Her Remarkable Career

No one knows exactly how many notches Helen Chenoweth has on her headboard, but one thing is for sure: she totally scored with the Big Guy.

"I've asked for God's forgiveness, and I've received it," she said.

What's all this forgiveness talk from a Republican? What do they need forgiveness for? Chenoweth, a two-term Republican representative from Idaho, was a major proponent of "family values": you know, marriage between a man and a woman, no abortion, no same-sex marriage . . . you get the picture. Chenoweth had reached the hallowed halls of the U.S. Capitol after taking up the mantle of her predecessor, Congressman Steve Symms, yet another stellar Republican brought down by sex scandals (who knew Boise was the American equivalent of Bangkok?).

Chenoweth's most loyal constituents were those like the John Birch Society, white supremacy groups, assorted militias, and nuts living on the frontier with only their guns, a bottle of moonshine, and the company of their personal demons. To the John Birch Society, which once accused President Dwight Eisenhower and Supreme Court Chief Justice Earl Warren of being Communist conspirators, Chenoweth offered this high praise: "Thank goodness for those, such as members of the John Birch Society, who are unashamed to advocate love of country, defense of our nation, and an abiding commitment to our constitution."

During her tenure as politician, Chenoweth also liked to bark about the evils of labor unions, and once said environmentalism was a pagan religion that should be banned from representation in government. Meanwhile, she endorsed her own religion using rationalization only a bigot could love:

"Regulatory and case law is the lowest form of law—God being the highest form of law."

And when she wasn't fighting to save us from freedom, equality, and forests, Chenoweth was voting to defend marriage.

## Her Personal Commitment

So there was this guy Vernon Ravenscroft, a man with a name as gothic as Chenoweth's own dogma, and he had a wife and a consulting firm. He also had a mistress named Helen Chenoweth. In 1998, Chenoweth admitted to having had a six-year affair with Ravenscroft in the 1980s. Though Chenoweth wasn't married at the time of the affair—like many Republicans who decry the erosion of family values in America due to the nefarious work of gays and liberals, Chenoweth was divorced—ol' Vern was not, and so the affair was adulterous.

This revelation could have been just another politician's peccadillo discussed over scotch at a Beltway bar; but when the affair was revealed, Chenoweth was currently ripping President Bill Clinton a new one for the infamous hummer he received in the Oval Office. "Our Founding Fathers knew that political leaders' personal conduct must be held to the highest standards," she said in campaign ads back in Idaho. Counting on the outrage among ordinary Americans in response to Clinton's philandering—outrage that never manifested itself despite the Republicans' and Kenneth Starr's best efforts—Chenoweth began to campaign on family values and character.

But no one asked Chenoweth about the alleged affair because it simply wasn't deemed relevant. Until it was. As Chenoweth was stepping on Clinton in order to get reelected, political reporters for the *Idaho Statesman* asked the representative about her rumored longtime liaison with our man Vern. She admitted to the liaison with the right-wing rancher.

"My private life is my own life," she told the paper. "I am a single woman. After the divorce I dated." Totally fair, Hel'. We feel you on that one. But it's the 'my private life is my own life' that we take issue with. It's a courtesy you don't extend to gays, for one, and presidents, for another.

Chenoweth gave herself props for admitting to the Ravenscroft affair when asked about it—something she said differentiated her from Papa Clinton. However, she'd actually denied the affair when she had been questioned about it by a Spokane newspaper reporter, Ken Olsen, years earlier. According to *Salon,* Olsen's notes from the interview quote Chenoweth as responding to the question this way: "For heaven's sakes, that is low. I'm utterly speechless. My official answer would have to be, this indicates a measure of desperation. People who know me know better than that. People who know Mr. Ravenscroft and his fine family know better than that."

In the fallout surrounding the scandal, Chenoweth begged for that very thing she was never willing to extend to Clinton, gays, welfare mothers, or anyone else she thought was going to hell: tolerance and forgiveness. She even ripped a page from Clinton's playbook: the family defense.

"Fourteen years ago, when I was a private citizen and a single woman, I was involved in a relationship that I came to regret, that I'm not proud of . . . This was in my past, and I'm very sorry . . . I very much regret that this once-private episode is now causing our families pain once more."

But don't tell that to Mrs. Ravenscroft. "I don't see how Helen can live with herself and do this," she told the *Statesman*.

In 2001, Chenoweth chose not to seek reelection.

MORALITY SCORE

**Attacks on a president who violated his wedding vows: countless. Campaigns run on a family values platform: two. Affairs with a married rancher from Idaho: one.**

# Reverend Sun Myung Moon

## MOONIE-IN-CHIEF

The head of the love organ is shaped exactly like a poisonous rattlesnake . . . and just like a rattlesnake, it's always looking for a hole. . . . If you misuse your love organ, you destroy life, your nation, and your world.

—*Rev. Sun Myung Moon, discussing homosexuals and childless couples*

## His Remarkable Career

Lots of contemporary conservatives are Moonies and don't even know it. The founder of the Unification Church, and one of the most notorious pseudo-Christian cultists of modern times, Sun Myung Moon started preaching in 1956. A little stew of Christianity, self-worship, and David Koresh, Moon's religion is built on the premise that he is an incarnation of God, put on this earth to finish Jesus' work. And when you see him on the street, call him "The Father." That's what he prefers to be called.

Throughout the years, former Moonies described the organization as a kind of cult. Once in, they were discouraged from contacting their friends or families and encouraged to "rise vertically" and join "Father Moon." The far right couldn't ask for a better collaborator.

Throughout the seventies, Moon's Moonies earned a reputation for annoying neighborhood canvasses, aggressive donation drives, and their hard sell when looking for new recruits. Meanwhile, Moon took care of the glamour work, befriending Republican presidents Richard Nixon and Gerald Ford.

In 1981, Moon was indicted for and convicted of tax evasion. It was the sixth time he'd been jailed, including one prior conviction for counterfeiting in South Korea. Jesus, it seems, was a petty white-collar criminal.

Not long after his imprisonment, Moon founded the *Washington Times*. The *Times* is heralded by many as the conservative foil to the *Washington Post*. Moon, in his infinite wisdom, also purchased the UPI news wire. On the occasion of the opening of Moon's Latin American newspaper, *Tiempos del Mundo*, former president George H. W. Bush delivered a speech, calling the *Washington Times* a paper that "brings sanity to Washington, D.C." (Besides Bush Sr., other Moony shadowers include Gerald Ford and Jerry Falwell.)

The *Washington Times* editorial page is an orgy of pro-Republican sycophancy, and the same-sex-marriage thing, well, that *really* gets under its skin. The day after the Massachusetts Supreme Court recognized same-sex marriage, the *Washington Times* expressed its contempt by putting every mention of same-sex marriage in quotation marks: "Homosexuals 'marry' in Massachusetts." And should you miss the subtle sarcasm, Moon's minions ran a staff editorial explaining the petty punctuation:

> The decision yesterday by the Massachusetts Supreme Court, by the margin of four to three, that homosexuals have the right to "marry" under that state's constitution could force all states to decide whether to recognize gay "marriage." The quotation marks around "marriage" are important. To those of us who believe that marriage is properly reserved for unions of one man and one woman it has become clear that, given current judicial trends, homosexual "marriage" is likely to become the law of the land without an amendment to the U.S. Constitution. President Bush, learning of the ruling as he landed yesterday in London, promised to work with legislative leaders to protect the sanctity of marriage as we have known it for centuries. This is good news.

The latest incarnation of Jesus, it seems, delivers the good news from all quarters: you can be saved through the body of Christ and marriage is really sacred and stuff.

Except that, despite the aggressive punctuation and all that talk of sanctity, Rev. Moon is not really all that good with marriage—or perhaps he's too good.

## His Personal Commitment

Aside from being a convict, Rev. Moon misused his "rattlesnake" at least once. In 1953, while still married to his first wife, Sung Gil Choi, Moon impregnated a university student, Myung Hee Kim. She bore him a son who died in a train wreck thirteen years later. By 1955, Moon was a divorcé.

When he's not fathering kids in extramarital affairs and getting divorces, Moon believes so fervently in maintaining the sanctity of marriage, in according it the respect it deserves, in taking it back from those who would make it a circus, that he performs thousands of them—simultaneously.

His biggest mass-marriage ceremony was in 1995, when he presided over the vows of 360,000 couples in Seoul, Korea. By popping out marriages faster than Hyundai builds Elantras, at least the heteros can maintain the lead over those marriage-minded homos.

Moon expected his newly married Moonies to produce more followers, and quickly; he even gives them explicit instructions in his religious texts:

Sex before marriage is out of the question, and when sexual consummation does happen, it must adhere to very specific instructions. First, a photograph of Moon must be nearby, so that everything occurs under the reverend's watchful eye. After two nights of woman-on-top sex, the couple reverse positions, whereupon the man, according to Moon, restores dominion over Eve, via the proper missionary position. Then, according to the instructions attributed to the U.C.'s American Blessed Family Department, "after the act of love, both spouses should wipe their sexual areas with the Holy Handkerchief"—referring to the church-supplied washcloth—which must "be kept individually labeled and should never be laundered or mixed up."

And the Republicans thought the blue dress was bad.

Moon continues to silently influence American right-wing politics. No one knows exactly how many front companies he owns, but his critics charge that he used soft money to influence and then market George W. Bush's 2000 primary campaign in North Carolina.

In 2003, at a ceremony in a Senate office building in Washington, D.C., a group of congressmen including Republicans Senator Lindsey Graham of South Carolina, Representative Roscoe Bartlett of Maryland, and Charlie Black, a top Republican strategist, attended the coronation of Moon and his wife. The pair even wore royal robes to the event, and Moon proclaimed himself to be "the second coming."

In 2004, the *San Francisco Chronicle* reported that the Bush administration had brought four "longtime operatives" of Moon's Unification Church on board and placed them on the federal payroll. Their roles? To strengthen Bush's Healthy Marriage Initiative.

MORALITY SCORE

Divorces: one. Convictions: six.
Divine wisdom: infinite.

# The
# Silent Majority

**Silence is the true friend that never betrays.**
*—Confucius*

ONE OF THE MOST RENOWNED Christian conservatives of modern times, Richard M. Nixon, coined the phrase "silent majority" to describe the everyday folks in America who worked hard, raised good, moral families, and who, in their hearts, supported the bombing of their Vietnamese counterparts, even if they didn't admit to it at PTA meetings. Their silence had repercussions—and gave a man directing an unjust war the political capital (and confidence) to continue the bloodshed.

Some three decades after Nixon defined the "silent majority," I've purloined the term to describe his moral descendants. Except these members of the silent majority aren't everyday Americans—they're a privileged class of (mostly) white (mostly) males who seek to modify the morality of others while doing whatever tickles their own slick willies. While they seek to work today's public into a far-from-silent fervor over a host of issues like deregulation, taxes, defense spending, and welfare reform, they fade into the background when the discussion turns to morality. Their votes and political bedfellows say one thing, but their actions behind locked hotel-room doors say another.

When fouling the marital bed, and maybe somebody else's, while working the public into a moralistic frenzy, a good strategy to keep it all sanctified is to keep your mouth shut.

# Representative Bill Thomas

## (R·CALIFORNIA)

## His Remarkable Career

I just flew in from Bakersfield, and boy, are my arms tired.

I was so poor, I got married for the rice.

I don't like political jokes. Too many of them get elected.

A congressman and a lady lobbyist meet on Capitol Hill . . .

What's the punch line of the last joke? Ask California Representative Bill Thomas: "Any personal failures of commitment or responsibility to my wife, family, or friends are just that, personal." He's a real funny guy, for all the wrong reasons. The buttoned-down Bakersfield Republican's hypocrisy would be a barrel of laughs if the implications weren't so grave.

He voted for term limits, but he's been in Congress for

nearly thirty years. (Cue canned laughter.) He once said that government was "too big, too intrusive, too easy with money" and was promptly named chair of the big, intrusive, easy with money Ways and Means Committee. (Cue rim shot.) He voted for the Defense of Marriage Act and allegedly cheated on his wife with a Beltway bimbo. (Cue groans.)

A strange fellow, Bill Thomas graduated from Santa Ana Community College before receiving a bachelor's and a master's from San Francisco State University, situated in the city of those-we-shall-defend-marriage-against. With his wife, Sharon, he fathered two kids. He became a nutty political science professor (seeing a pattern here?), and then an oddball politician. The *Washington Post*'s Mark Leibovich described the congressman's personality quirks this way:

> Thomas has the fidgety manner of an overgrown boy (one who chews unlit cigars). He is prone to radical swings of tone and subject. One former staffer recalls a phone call from Thomas that began as a stream-of-consciousness lecture on some legislative arcana. It segued into a burst of uproarious laughter and culminated in an out-of-nowhere tantrum that ended with Thomas saying the aide had just uttered "the stupidest thing [Thomas] had ever heard." The congressman then slammed down the phone. The call lasted two minutes.

Thomas was a nutty rambler and a guy who might do well to take a Tony Robbins workshop. And yet, interestingly, his voting patterns remained consistent: consistently oppressive and consistently repressive. He became one of those quiet Republicans who let the Blowhards, Self-Loathers, and Wily Evaders take the flak while he, by his votes, advanced their agenda. In addition to voting for the Defense of Marriage Act, Thomas voted for a federal amendment to the Constitution banning gays from marrying.

This antigovernment paragon who had been in government since Methuselah has received failing grades by nearly every think tank in town. Except from the NRA, which gave him an A.

The chagrined professor received only a 76 percent approval rating from the Christian Coalition. Why would this good Republican, committed to preserving the sanctity of marriages across the country, be docked almost 25 percent from his good boy score? Could it have been because he was caught with a woman who wasn't his partner in the holy institution of marriage? Although Bill Thomas is anti–health care, he does favor heath-care lobbyists.

## His Personal Commitment

Bill Thomas has taken refuge in the silent majority haven for good reason. Talk about morality from a guy who is confused about morality (at least his own—he's pretty clear about what others' morality ought to look like) is a little hard to stomach. So, although he's vociferous on the topic of rising health-care costs, the evils of labor unions, and the importance of military bases, Thomas shrinks back into the shadows when talk turns to the question of morality. But hypocrites aren't known by their words alone: they let their votes do the talking.

In July of 2000, scarcely two years after the House Republicans attempted to uproot a president for questionable morality and conflict-of-interest issues (while dubbing him "Slick Willy"), the *Bakersfield Californian* ran a front-page headline that read "The Congressman and the Lobbyist." No, it wasn't the title of a bad joke. It was just the beginning of a long article detailing an alleged affair the Republican congressman had had with a lobbyist. The photo accompanying the article showed Thomas grinning like a nerdy guy sleeping with a cute lobbyist, and impressing the ladies with an ugly tie given him by another stellar Republican, former drug addict and veteran divorcé Rush Limbaugh.

The article described an "intensely personal relationship" between Thomas and Deborah Steelman, a health-care lobbyist who had spent considerable time with Thomas's health-care committee in Congress, and had also been responsible for stuffing Thomas's coffers with big campaign donations. The married Thomas and the equally married Steelman honored their marriages by taking to each other's arms. Cut the guy a break—it must have been hard to resist, given what the two had in common: she was the leading health-care industry lobbyist and he chaired the Ways and

Means Committee, including the health-care finance sub-committee. They were positively *made* for each other.

As Thomas and Steelman were fluffing the pillows, Thomas, ever the policy geek, devised a plan to provide prescription drug benefits to Medicare recipients. The change of heart—from steely opposition to increasing health-care costs to government to bleeding-heart-liberal-style charity—was moving. Even more inspiring to the lobbying community was the $3 million Steelman collected from her health-care industry clients, according to Public Citizen, during that time.

Forget oil for food. We've found something better. Oh, except that Steelman, who didn't deny the affair, was just steamed at the idea that anyone would think she used her body to gain legislative flavors—sorry, favors. "To suggest that I would stoop to an 'inappropriate relationship' to achieve legislative results is repugnant and sexist."

Bill Thomas refused to confirm or deny the affair, but did pull that line about his personal life being personal (as opposed to the personal lives of those millions whose sexuality he legislated against—but that's just semantics). The *Californian* cited Thomas's chief of staff, Cathy Abernathy, as the one spilling the beans to associates about Thomas's trysts. Evidently, she was concerned that the public might be upset about Thomas hopping into bed with industry.

Thomas said the relationship created no conflict of interest. But people not sleeping with married lobbyists while writing legislation were of another mind.

Incidentally, Thomas received nearly $57,000 from drug companies for his most recent campaign, more than any other candidate in the House (word gets around quickly). For her part, Steelman chipped in the federal limit of two thousand dollars for the congressman's campaign, as well as a three-thousand-dollar donation to his leadership committee.

Say what you will, but Bill Thomas was no cheap date. If it's true that Thomas and Steelman reveled in hot, illicit love and even hotter legislative skullduggery, then the message sent to Thomas's fellow legislators may have been this: if you're going to sell your country to Big Pharma anyway, you might as well get a little on the side. As you're getting off, recall that you've canceled out your moral transgression by supporting the Defense of Marriage Act and casting a yes vote for the constitutional amendment. Protect marriage until death do you part, or until industry execs send you a cute blonde.

Is this thing on?

> ### MORALITY SCORE
>
> **Health-care plans sold: one. Wives wronged: one. Lobbyists befriended: one. Votes denying gays the right to marry: two.**

# Representative Dan Burton

## (R·INDIANA)

## His Remarkable Career

Representative Dan Burton used to be one of the nois-iest champions of family values on Capitol Hill. He worried about the decline of the American family; for single mothers and abused children, believing that bootstraps were for pulling, he positively seethed good old Indiana morality; he voted against "entitlements." A handsome devil, Burton represents Indiana's Sixth District and has long supported a fundamentalist conservative Christian platform; his favorite campaign slogan is "Character matters."

Burton hails from that bastion of conservatism in Middle America, Indianapolis. Born in 1938 to a former cop, Charles, and a waitress, Bonnie, Burton grew up poor. He spent most of his youth in trailer parks and motel rooms, watching his father regularly beat his mother. When Burton was twelve, his parents finally divorced—but then Charles kidnapped Bonnie at gunpoint and held her hostage for ten days. The Burton kids went to an orphanage for a short period of time. Like Bill Clinton, whom Burton called "a scumbag," Burton, then a teenager, faced off with his father (in Clinton's case it was his stepfather) with a shotgun and ran him off.

Burton attended Indiana University and, after enlisting in the Army in 1956, he moved on to the Cincinnati Bible Seminary, leaving without a degree. He moved on to another racket following his departure from the seminary—insurance. There he met his wife, to whom he's been married for nearly forty years. (Don't applaud yet.)

Voters first elected Burton to the Hoosier state house in 1967, when he was only twenty-eight years old. He subsequently ran for Congress twice, failing both times. Third time was the charm, and in 1982, Burton was elected to the United States Congress.

With a mother who raised him in a single-parent household and a childhood riddled with abuse, some misguided souls, journalist Russ Baker suggested in *Salon,* might conclude that Dan Burton would be a champion for single mothers, for children in abusive families, for the funding of child protective services. Although he's not an official Self-Loather, Burton's politics reflect a little self-hatred. He consistently votes to deny social services to disadvantaged children, believing that social "entitlements" cause nothing but trouble.

Burton's antieducation, antiminority, antiprogress, antigay, (but pro-gun) voting record has earned him a whopping 7 percent approval rating from the ACLU on human-rights issues.

In 1996, Burton began his job as a full-time Clinton hater as chair of the House Committee on Government Reform. In fact, Burton was one of the key Clinton drumbeaters, impeaching the president's moral character verbally, but also literally: Burton concocted the idea that the Clinton administration offed Vince Foster, and publicly demonstrated his hypothesis with a rifle and a watermelon.

In 1996, Burton voted for the Defense of Marriage Act. In 2004, he (unlike a number of less sanctimonious pricks who voted for DOMA but stopped short of actually trying to write oppression into the constitution) voted for the Federal Marriage Amendment.

Because character matters.

## His Personal Commitment

No one, regardless of what party they serve, no one, regardless of what branch of government they serve, should be allowed to get away with these alleged sexual improprieties.

— *Dan Burton, September 13, 1995,*
*addressing Congress*

If I could prove ten percent of what I believe happened, he'd be gone. This guy's a scumbag. That's why I'm after him.

—*Dan Burton, on Bill Clinton*
*to the* Indianapolis Star

"During part of the 1970s and '80s, Dan Burton was known as the biggest skirt-chaser in the Indiana legislature," *Indianapolis Star* reporter Dick Cady wrote. "Lobbyists whispered about the stories of Burton's escapades . . . to the people who sent him first to the legislature and then to Congress, Burton was Mr. Conservative, the devout husband and father who espoused family values."

But Dan attends Indianapolis's 91st Street Christian Church!

"For a man who claims to be such a moralist," one journalist quipped at the Indianapolis Press Club's roast of Burton, "Danny does have a reputation as a ladies' man. He is all for life, liberty, and the happiness of pursuit."

But Dan is a "born-again Christian"! He's even earned a 100 percent approval rating from the Christian Coalition!

"She was most embarrassed when he propositioned her," former Republican state senator Virginia Blankenbaker recalled of her intern, a young woman Burton had his eye on. "It's bizarre he's so outspoken on moral issues."

But Dan believes in the sanctity of marriage—he even

voted for a constitutional amendment that protects it by banning same-sex marriage!

In 1998, Dan Burton announced publicly that he had fathered a child out of wedlock, while he was married, and that he'd been supporting the child financially but had no contact with him. The announcement was a preemptive move on Burton's part, who was anticipating an excoriating *Vanity Fair* article by investigative journalist Russ Baker, who had interviewed more than 120 sources about the congressman's checkered past. The article never ran in *Vanity Fair* (it was later published by *Salon*). But publications across the country picked up the tired old stories of Burton's womanizing (tired and old to Indianapolis and Washington politicians and reporters who were very familiar with the congressman's exploits but chose never to write about it).

He staffed them in the office! He put them on the payroll! He sought them out on the Hill! He invited them into his offices (and to dinner)! Women—young, nubile women!

Hurley Goodall, an old retired Democrat from the Indiana legislature, told Baker: "None of the [female] staff wanted to be caught in a hall with him." That's because when in the presence of a young female staffer, Burton got all touchy-feely.

"He put his hand on the back of my neck and said, 'Would your husband, your boyfriend, be upset about you being here late with me tonight?'" one woman told Baker. In 1983, Burton promoted a woman named Rebecca Hyatt from babysitter to "assistant to the administrative assistant" in his Washington office, and, according to Hyatt's ex-husband, took advantage of political privilege, conducting an affair with the young woman.

But Dan Burton voted to ban gay adoptions, indicating his very great dedication to salvaging the divine institution of heterosexual marriage and the dignity of the American family!

In the 1990s, during what Planned Parenthood knew would be a fruitless lobbying visit, three delegates, two men and a woman (who was also a Republican), were ushered in to a tiny closet-size room in Dan Burton's Washington office. The meeting began with Burton waxing rhapsodic about his seminary years. When they realized the meeting was going nowhere, the delegates decided to leave. As the two male delegates passed out of the doorway, Burton stood aside to make room for them, but when the female delegate tried to leave, Burton, according to the woman in question, "grabbed my arm and pulled me back . . . he had his hands up my skirt so fast I didn't even know what was coming."

But Burton is all for women's lib—in fact, he sees to it that much of his staff is female, including a former campaign manager, Claudia Keller. Who said models are stupid? Not this one. She's so capable that she was able to run Burton's congressional campaigns out of her Indianapolis home, often greeting her boss in a teddy. (Didn't James Carville do that, too?)

Dan Burton continues to vigorously defend the institution of marriage and the old-fashioned morality that made this country great as he leads by example.

## MORALITY SCORE

ACLU civil rights rating: 7 percent. Christian Coalition rating: 100 percent. Votes to ban same-sex marriage: two. Wives: one. Models: one. Illegitimate children resulting from an adulterous affair: one. Shame: none.

# Senator Strom Thurmond

## (R-SOUTH CAROLINA, DECEASED)

We regard the decisions of the Supreme Court in the school cases as a clear abuse of judicial power. It climaxes a trend in the Federal Judiciary undertaking to legislate, in derogation of the authority of Congress, and to encroach upon the reserved rights of the States and the people.

*—Strom Thurmond's 1956 "Southern Manifesto" endorsing racial segregation*

We believe that the self-proclaimed supremacy of these judicial activists is antithetical to the democratic ideals on which our nation was founded. President Bush has established a solid record of nominating only judges who have demonstrated respect for the Constitution and the democratic processes of our republic.

*—The official 2004 GOP platform*

# His Remarkable Career

In 2004, fifty years after *Brown v. Board of Education,* Republicans rephrased Thurmond's incendiary language when they tried to revive their socially conservative causes, outlaw abortion, and permanently ban same-sex marriage.

Senator Strom Thurmond was born in 1902, and they say he died in 2003, though if you had seen him being literally wheeled around the Capitol in those last years, you'd have been hard pressed to determine whether he was still among the living.

As a young bigot, Thurmond attended Clemson University, which was then Clemson College. By 1938, he was a county attorney and a state senator until his appointment to the circuit court. But when the war came, he dropped his gavel, grabbed a rifle, and landed at Normandy with the 82nd Airborne. After he helped beat back the white supremacists in Europe, he served briefly in the Pacific before returning to South Carolina, where he successfully ran for governor in 1947.

In 1948, Strom publicly objected to the Democratic Party's nomination of Harry Truman, and Thurmond decided to give it a go himself, running on the States' Rights Democratic Party ticket—also known as the segregationist Dixiecrats. Thurmond once told his followers, "All the bayonets in the Army cannot force the Negro into our homes, our schools, our churches and our places of recreation." (Fifty years later, though, we can't keep Southern governors out of our bedrooms.) Thurmond's racist dogma won the hearts of voters—and electors—of four present-day red states: Louisiana, Alabama, Mississippi, and South Carolina. In 1956, he penned "The Southern Manifesto," a frothing objection to Supreme Court desegregation.

Then, in 1957, he set another political record: longest filibuster. Thurmond spent twenty-four hours, eighteen minutes on the Senate floor speaking against a civil rights act allowing black citizens to vote.

Now that's dedication.

Thurmond, like Jesse Helms and other old-school Southern bigots, realized the Democrats weren't concerned enough about preserving the sanctity of Jim Crow, and Lyndon Johnson's support of the '64 Civil Rights Act was the last straw. Thurmond became a Republican. And then, in the beginning volley of the Republicans' long, arduous battle for the reinstatement of family values in everyday life, Thurmond, a sixty-six-year-old widower, married a twenty-two-year-old pageant queen.

If you had seen Thurmond being wheeled around by aides during the last decade of his life, you might've felt bad for the old son of a gun: his aides had to help him cast his votes, they had to help him use the toilet, etc. But before you let your liberal compassion get the best of you, consider that

Thurmond was still ordering his aides to push every button possible to oppress minorities. He voted for Bob Barr's Defense of Marriage Act, voted against the legalization of same-sex marriage and against adding sexual orientation to the definition of "hate crime," a label he opposed when it was used to define racial crimes.

## His Personal Commitment

Strom Thurmond—Baptist, Racist, and Christian Ideologue (we think it said this on his business cards)—upheld the standards of good Christian living by fathering a baby out of wedlock. Oh, yeah, a biracial baby.

Thurmond's daughter, Essie Mae Washington-Williams, did the Christian thing and waited until after her father's death before coming forward. Washington-Williams, the daughter of Thurmond and a former Thurmond maid, was born in 1925. She later moved to Pennsylvania with her mother, and had never even met Thurmond until she was a teenager, when her mother took Essie to Thurmond's law offices.

Thurmond paid Essie's tuition at South Carolina State University, and although rumors circulated about their relationship for decades, the rumors were never confirmed until after Thurmond's untimely death.

Bennettsville lawyer Frank E. Cain, a college classmate of Essie's, told *The Black Commentator* there was nothing atypical about Thurmond's stewardship of an African-American at a time when Strom was pushing racist legislation and calling people "niggers."

"It's just a carry-over from slavery where the white land-lord had his black family," Cain said. "That's the old South."

The moral of the story: There's a racist in every wood-pile. If federal troops and social upheaval force the accept-ance of one group, find another one to oppress. It's okay to screw your black maid, but not your gay hairdresser.

> ## MORALITY SCORE
>
> **Consecutive hours spent blocking civil rights legislation: twenty-four. Votes to defend marriage: one. Black children fathered by Thurmond while he was unmarried: one.**

# Michael Bowers

**Former Attorney General
for the State of Georgia**

## His Remarkable Career

Y ou can't hold former Georgia Attorney General Michael Bowers down, son. He's got a JD, an MBA, an MS, and BS. But of course, down South, BS isn't just a political commodity—it's an art form.

Bowers was elected by the populace of Georgia to the attorney general's office in 1981. Five years later, Bowers successfully argued the validity of criminal sodomy laws before the U.S. Supreme Court, and the decision stood for more than a decade before the judges sobered up. The trouble started in 1982, when the door to Michael Hardwick's bedroom door came flying open as he was engaged in oral sex with another man. The door-flinger was an Atlanta police officer.

Rewind a bit. Hardwick, a bartender at a gay club, left work carrying a beer one night. He tossed it in a garbage can outside, but a policeman cited him for public drinking anyway. Hardwick missed the court date because his ticket listed the wrong date for his appearance. However, he paid the fine—and was arrested anyway, at three in the morning at his apartment, in his bedroom with his boyfriend. Suddenly, that beer didn't seem so important to the Atlanta police department.

The two men were arrested and charged with sodomy. In Georgia, sodomy—a term that covers all oral and anal sexual relations—was a punishable offense. You could do hard time for it, up to twenty years in the International House o' Sodomy—prison.

At the time, twenty-four states still had laws on the books that made sodomy a criminal offense. Nineteen of those states—including Georgia—banned anal and oral intercourse. Five states specifically prohibited homosexual acts.

Interestingly, the law was as flexible as a Barnum & Bailey's contortionist—for some folks. Oral sex—even extramarital oral sex—was perfectly legal for Hardwick's fellow Georgian Newt Gingrich. It was a prosecutable offense for Michael Hardwick. We're guessing it's because Hardwick was gay (or a man not involved in making federal legislation regarding the private lives of others—could be either one).

But Hardwick never got a chance to ply the Newt Defense. Initially, the local district attorney chose not to pursue the charges. However, Hardwick and his lawyers were outraged, and had their eyes on the United States Supreme Court, with the hopes of challenging the very constitutionality of the Georgia sodomy law. While the District Court dismissed the challenge, the U.S. Court of Appeals heard the case and reversed the ruling. For one, brief shining moment, an individual's right to privacy was considered sacred.

But along came Bowers. The Georgia attorney general caught wind of this act of moral and judicial cowardice and grabbed on to the *Hardwick* case with the tenacity with which a pit bull grabs on to a toddler's leg.

Back in the mid-eighties, the U.S. Supreme Court was not the progressive, youthful, and open-minded organ it is now, and Bowers successfully defended the anti-sodomy statute. Justice Byron White, writing for the majority, said the idea that homosexuals had a right to privacy was "factitious." On the bright, but losing, side, justices Harry Blackmun and John Paul Stevens were vehement in their dissents. Justice Blackmun wrote that "a State can no more punish private behavior because of religious intolerance than it can punish such behavior because of racial animus."

Bowers basked in the victory, though. Score one for family values. The sinners were caught in flagrante delicto. But the boy genius of BS wasn't done with the gays yet.

Eleven years after the *Hardwick* decision, the pious attorney general again found himself at the defense table, this time for reversing a job offer to attorney Robin Shahar after learning she was going to participate in a commitment ceremony with her female lover. In *Shahar v. Bowers,* Shahar claimed discrimination and violation of her freedom of speech. Shockingly, the Georgia courts found in Bowers's favor, and the U.S. Supreme Court declined to review the case.

And all was well with the world: the Republican attorney general had beaten back the activist judges, the liberals, the gays, and had preserved the law of the land.

All was right with the world, until the golden boy's shiny paint flaked off.

## His Personal Commitment

I n 1997, Mike Bowers ran for governor of Georgia. It seemed the natural next step: he'd spent more than fifteen years keeping Georgia focused on God, family values, and that Confederate flag. Add to that impressive résumé of moral battles won a major generalship in the Air National Guard, and you had a shoo-in candidate for the governorship of Georgia.

Oh. Except that that generalship in the Air National Guard? Yeah, he had to resign his Air Force commission. That's because in the military, adultery is a crime.

Before kicking off his campaign for governor, Bowers publicly admitted that he had committed adultery for ten years, all the way back to the time when he passionately argued Georgia's morals laws in front of the supreme court of the land—when he noted in his defense that in Georgia, adultery is a misdemeanor.

Bowers, who was married, had taken another's bride; his lover was a state employee who, at the beginning of their tryst, anyway, was married. Bowers never indicated whether or not his lover "gave good sodomy," but one can only imagine. Somehow, Bowers managed to keep his wife, but lost his voters. He contributes to the Republican cause these days as a litigator at Balch & Bingham LLP of Atlanta. So much for beating back the "litigious culture."

Twelve years after *Bowers v. Hardwick,* the Georgia Supreme Court finally struck down the state's 182-year-old sodomy law, citing the right to privacy guaranteed by the state's constitution. Bowers had no comment.

> ## MORALITY SCORE
>
> **Condemnations of gays that masqueraded as cases made for morality: two. Adulterous affairs: one. Gubernatorial races lost: one.**

# Bill O'Reilly

## CONSERVATIVE TALK-SHOW HOST

## His Remarkable Career

**B**ill O'Reilly blows harder than almost any blowhard in the world, but he's strangely oblique when it comes to same-sex marriage (even if his talk-show guests are not).

O'Reilly claims he's the son of a working-class family from the original suburb, Levittown, New York. This blue-collar background, however, has been rejected by O'Reilly's opponents, who point out that the talk-show host attended the prestigious boys' high school Chaminade. O'Reilly also attended Marist College, Boston University, and Harvard's Kennedy School of Government. He has a pair of Emmys for excellence in reporting won while practicing local journalism in Denver and, later, for CBS, honors that led him, naturally, to *Hard Copy,* a show that did for news what *Baywatch* did for serious prime-time television.

The big day came when Fox needed another vocal supporter for their public service department (Divisions of Election Derailing and Spouting of Republican Dogma and Calling It Objective News). Once comfortably seated behind the desk, O'Reilly followed the Limbaugh tradition of "If it's loud, it must be true." The "Fair and Balanced" network's "no-spin" commentator racked up multiple years atop the ratings charts, launching best-selling books and a successful radio show, all by riding a hard-line of conservatism and moral outrage.

## His Personal Commitment

In a book about marriage and old, rich men trying to bang the help, O'Reilly fits right in (or: allegedly fits right in). On October 14, 2004, O'Reilly and Fox filed suit against associate producer Andrea Mackris for trying to extort "hush money" from O'Reilly and the company. That same day, Mackris filed a countersuit for a whopping $60 million.

What an ungrateful bitch. This, after O'Reilly offered Mackris a Caribbean vacation! So what if he wanted to tag along? His wife and two kids would understand that papa had work to do. Work like painting vivid scenes for Mackris (later quoted in her lawsuit):

> You would basically be in the shower, and then I would—and then I would come in and I'd join you and you would have your back to me and I would take that little loofah thing and

kinda' soap up your back . . . rub it all over you, get you to relax, hot water . . . and um . . . you know, you'd feel the tension drain out of you and, uh, you still would be with your back to me then I would kinda' put my arm—it's one of those mitts, those loofah mitts you know, so I got my hands in it . . . and I would put it around front, kinda' rub your tummy a little bit with it and then with my other hand I would start to massage your boobs, get your nipples really hard . . . 'cuz I like that, and you have really spectacular boobs . . .

For someone who's so articulate on television, something's sure got O'Reilly tongue-tied. And Mackris? Jesus, how did she resist the image of a naked Bill O'Reilly coming at her with a soapy loofah sponge!

So the Caribbean didn't work out. What about Italy? Or Thailand? According to Mackris's papers, O'Reilly's been known to score in such exotic locales:

. . . During the course of this dinner, in approximately May 2003, Defendant Bill O'Reilly, without solicitation or invite, regaled plaintiff and her friend with stories concerning the loss of his virginity to a girl in a car at JFK, two "really wild" Scandinavian airline stewardesses he had gotten together with, and a "girl" at a sex show in Thailand who had shown him things in a back room that "blew [his] mind." Defendant then stated he was going to Italy to meet the Pope, that his pregnant wife was staying at home with his daughter, and implied he was looking forward to some extramarital dalliances with the "hot" Italian women. Both Plaintiff and her friend were repulsed, but felt powerless to protest strongly since Defendant was Plaintiff's boss . . .

O'Reilly's suit against Mackris, which was filed hours before Mackris's suit, claimed the former producer was extorting him. Although his lawyers, in a triumph of alliteration, called Mackris's charges "scurrilous and scandalous," they never denied them.

These days, when he's not railing against the liberals (or enjoying his loofah sponge), O'Reilly writes kids' books. In his book *The O'Reilly Factor for Kids: A Survival Guide for American Families,* O'Reilly offered advice for dealing with challenging situations. It did not include this piece of advice he once doled out to a younger person: ". . . Defendant Bill O'Reilly said to Plaintiff Andrea Mackris: 'And just use your vibrator to blow off steam.'"

## MORALITY SCORE

**Televised conservative rants: too many to count. Images that can never be scrubbed clean from your brain: one. $60 million harassment suits settled out of court: one.**

# Self-Loathers
# and Wily Evaders

**I hate myself for loving you.**
*—Joan Jett and the Blackhearts*

## Self-Loathers

THE SACRIFICE WAS GREAT, and the cause worth lying for. The following politicians, journalists, and other members of the Anti–Gay Marriage Fan Club courageously set aside their sexuality—in some cases, denied it—in order that the Republicans might conquer and divide. Boldly concealing their own sexualities in order to regulate others', the Self-Loathers successfully punished their own folk with regressive legislation. Thanks to their efforts, their gay brethren cannot make a public and federally recognized commitment of their relationships.

# Wily Evaders

Then there are the Wily Evaders, those slippery devils who won't confirm, who won't deny, and who won't be held accountable. They are crafty folk who, by keeping mum about their own tendencies, avoid the political skillet, and, instead, are the ones sautéing whole segments of the population. Some dirty liberals might have assumed that the Self-Loathers' friends in the health-care lobby would have provided them with enough Zoloft to prevent such cannibalism. Interestingly, those same dirty liberals—the ones with the hearts soiling their sleeves—might wonder if one's sexuality is relevant to a discussion about legislation. Gay activist John Aravosis, one of the main architects of the congressional outing campaign that took place on blogs across the country and, later, major newspapers, justified his motives this way: "If you're gay and you support making sexual orientation a political weapon, then your sexual orientation is fair game."

This section documents the activities of those who can be categorized as Self-Loathers if they have officially come out of the closet (or have been forced out) and those called Wily Evaders, around whom speculation swirls, but who refuse to comment on their own sexualities, even as they legislate sexual politics.

Democratic congressman and one of the only openly gay men on Capitol Hill Barney Frank said that he wasn't inclined to out legislators unless the congressman in question was rabidly antigay. However, he said, "You don't have a right to be a hypocrite; you don't have a right to exempt yourself from the negative things you do to other people."

# Representative Ed Schrock

## (R·VIRGINIA, RESIGNED)

You're in the showers with them! You're in the bunk room with them, you're in staterooms with them!

—*Ed Schrock, explaining his disapproval of Bill Clinton's "Don't Ask, Don't Tell" military policy*

## His Remarkable Career

In 2000, Conservative Republican Ed Schrock came to the U.S. House of Representatives with faith in God and secrets in his closet. He was six-feet-four, two hundred pounds, very muscular, very buffed, with blond hair and—oh, wait, that's from his unofficial biography, which we'll get to shortly.

Representative Schrock was a shining star in the Republican caucus, voted president of the Republican freshman class of 2000 due to his ultra-tight abs. Sorry. Due to his ultraconservative views and voting record. Schrock sat on several committees, including the House Armed Services Committee, and founded a committee of his own to address navy and marine corps issues. His stated purpose in the House was to make government smaller, and less intrusive into the private lives of its citizens. Except those citizens who happen to be gay.

Representative Schrock was a staunch social conservative, as well as a Baptist, with a voting record so pristinely conservative that the Christian Coalition gave him a 92 percent approval rating. Schrock, a Vietnam vet and retired Navy officer, represented a district that included nine military bases (and Pat Robertson's Regent University). When Bill Clinton's "Don't Ask, Don't Tell" policy was brought back into debate, legislation aimed at curbing discrimination, harassment, and assaults against gays in the military, Schrock was perhaps the most vocal opponent of the policy, shrieking, "You're in the showers with them! You're in the bunk room with them, you're in staterooms with them!" If you know Schrock's story, though, it might be hard to guess whether he was raising an alarm here or articulating a fantasy.

Regardless, Schrock claimed to be morally outraged at the idea of allowing gays to volunteer to fight for the country, and favored asking enlistees point blank if they'd had homosexual sex.

In case anyone was uncertain about where he stood on such matters, Schrock cosponsored the Federal Marriage Amendment, which would permanently outlaw same-sex marriage. He also voted for the Marriage Protection Act, which bars courts from legalizing same-sex marriage at both the state and the federal level.

Schrock may have wanted to protect his own marriage—to a retired schoolteacher who had borne him a son—from the gays. But it was too late.

## His Personal Commitment

**R**ep. Schrock's complaints about gays were nowhere near as graphic as the descriptions he left of himself on gay dating phone lines:

"Uh, hi, I weigh two hundred pounds, I'm six-four [inaudible] blond hair . . . very muscular, very buffed up, uh, very tanned, uh, I just like to get together with a guy from time to time, just to, just to play. I'd like him to be in very good shape, flat stomach, good chest, good arms, well hung, cut, uh, just get naked, play, and see what happens, nothing real heavy duty, but just, fun time, go down on him, he can go down on me, and just take it from there . . . hope to hear from you. Bye."

There were seven of these, all with slight variation on the same themes. One said he didn't want anything "hard core" because the situation required "discretion." Read: "I'm a big old liar and my Baptist buddies will run me out if they find out what I'm into."

During Schrock's 2004 reelection campaign, as the good congressman was running on a platform that included antigay legislation, gay activists and a blogger named Mike Rogers outed Schrock for being a naughty, naughty congressman. Those who made these tapes public claimed their motives were not to force another homosexual out of the closet; instead, it was to reveal the hypocrisy of some conservative Republicans whose own self-loathing led to legislation on a large scale—legislation that affects millions of happy, open-about-their-sexuality people—that is borne of that very personal, very individual self-loathing. Schrock, like many of the leaders profiled in this book, wanted to persecute people for doing the very things he engaged in secretly.

And let's not forget that Schrock was also married, with a child. Add some hot and bothered phone solicitations to the mix, and you have a hypocrisy stew that even Newt Gingrich might find hard to swallow.

What did this staunch champion of the (heterosexual) people do when confronted with these nefarious rumors—later confirmed—of hypocrisy? He beat a hasty retreat.

"After much thought and prayer," Schrock said in a statement, "I have come to the realization that these allegations will not allow my campaign to focus on the real issues facing our nation and region."

Gay-related issues used as a political tool to polarize voters? Unheard of.

Schrock was instantly replaced by another Republican. In keeping with the Republican adultery-makes-you-a-bad-person-only-if-you're-a-Democrat philosophy, the good Reverend Robertson was more than willing to forgive Schrock's slap and tickle.

"He is a wonderful congressman and a good personal friend," Robertson said. "I am deeply saddened at his decision to leave the House of Representatives. I do hope that he would find it in his heart to reconsider this abrupt decision in his life."

## MORALITY SCORE

**Anti–same sex marriage votes: two. Suspiciously fervent denunciations of "Don't Ask, Don't Tell" policy: one. Explicit gay dating phone recordings: seven.**

# Jeff Gannon
# (aka James Guckert)

**Fake News Reporter, Right-Wing Cheerleader**

President Bush stands to benefit by taking a
stand to protect traditional marriage.
— *Jeff Gannon, commenting on same-sex marriage
in a "news story" he authored, February 5, 2004*

Kerry Could Become First Gay President
— *Headline written by Jeff Gannon,
October 12, 2004*

## His Remarkable Career

**M**any administrations have hit the sheets with the
media, but they usually steer clear of prostitutes.
Not the Bush administration—in fact, its penchant is for the
male persuasion. Jeff Gannon may be the first gigolo ever
formally invited to the White House.

Jeff Gannon—his real name is James Dale Guckert—
spent two years in the presidential press pool, and despite all

that good-natured backslapping among colleagues, and their wry asides, very little else is known about him.

With a résumé that included such occupations as truck driver and schoolteacher, Gannon began covering the White House in February 2003 for an online magazine called *Talon News*. He was also working for a more straightforwardly named online publication called *GOPUSA*. Both journalistic entities were funded by a Republican activist from Texas named Bobby Eberle.

When he started reporting, Gannon changed his name from James Dale Guckert to Jeff Gannon because, according to him, his real name is hard to spell, and hard to pronounce. His bio on the *Talon News* Web site (the Web site has since erased every mention of their former intrepid reporter) mentioned that Gannon was a graduate of "the Pennsylvania state university system" and that he had also graduated from the "Leadership Institute Broadcast School of Journalism" (an institute proclaiming "conservative leaders, organizations, and activists rely on the Institute for the preparation they require for success").

Gannon was known for his friendly, softball questions during White House press conferences, his pro-Bush reporting, and his anti–same sex marriage comments. Gannon came into the White House press pool at a time when the Bush administration was secretly paying conservative journalists, columnists, and other pundits to praise Bush initiatives. Some of Gannon's press pool peers became suspicious of Gannon's sweet-as-pie questioning during press briefings; on more than one occasion, they reported Press Secretary Scott McClellan or even George W. Bush calling on Gannon after particularly pointed questions from journalists about serious issues. Gannon, it seems, could be relied upon to cool things off with a question about Democrats like: "How are you going to work with people who seem to have divorced themselves from reality?"

Many of Gannon's stories were on gay issues—during the 2004 presidential election, he detailed what he called John Kerry's "pro-homosexual platform," including a head-line that read "Kerry Could Become First Gay President." In reporting on Senator Rick Santorum's comments that legal-izing same-sex marriage would lead to the legalization of bestiality, Gannon isolated the comments of outraged gay activists as "predictable responses."

What was even more interesting was what his colleagues at GOPUSA were writing. Take Jimmy Moore, for a shrill example:

The unashamed and in-your-face activists involved in the gay agenda, the millions of people, including children as young as twelve, having sex outside the sanctity of marriage, multitudes of married men and women who are actively engaged in adultery, the spread of pornography, especially on the Internet, and many other forms of sexual perversion have sent our country on a one-way ticket to destruction.

The press pool piranhas, which had long been defanged by Bush, decided to eat one of their own. The reporters and the bloggers went to work, and what they found was almost an exact enactment of what Jimmy Moore warned his readers was a one-way ticket to hell.

## His Personal Commitment

Before he became a born-again Christian, a pseudonymous partisan cheerleader disguised as a reporter, and a "voice of the media so feared by the Left that it had to take me down," Jeff Gannon was featured, not in any prominent newspapers, but on such family values–oriented Web sites as Hotmilitarystud.com, Militaryescorts.com, and MilitaryEscortsM4M.com.

Gay activist John Aravosis of Americablog.org noticed that this young conservative—he called himself "Bulldog" in apparent reference to his past as a marine—was all over the Internet, in various states of undress. He even had his own site, in which he proffered his services as an escort. Gannon had also contracted with a Web developer to build a site that featured nude pictures of the pseudo-journalist (okay, not completely nude—he was wearing dog tags). On the site, he explained that he was an "aggressive top" who didn't "leave marks, just impressions."

When the reports started circulating on the Internet,

Gannon shrugged them off, saying he'd been hired by a private client to do some Web work. It wasn't long, though, before mainstream newspapers like the *Washington Post* picked up the story. In addition to his shady past as a pinup boy, Gannon's access to the White House came under the microscope: how was it that he gained access to the press room when *Talon News* was not a legitimate news source, but was, instead, a house organ of the far right wing?

In response, Scott McClellan announced that Gannon had gained access to the White House not as a representative of *Talon News,* but as a reporter for the notably nonobjective GOPUSA.com. McClellan said Gannon had forwarded his request for access on GOPUSA stationery. In other words, the administration admitted Gannon to the White House press pool knowing he didn't work for a news agency. Even worse, the *Washington Post* announced that Gannon had been the only reporter who had access to the infamously leaked CIA memo naming Valerie Plame as a covert CIA operative before conservative columnist Robert Novak exposed her. (For those who don't know, outing an undercover CIA agent is a felony; outing a pro-Bush hagiographer, on the other hand, is perfectly legal.)

With access like that, it seemed like Guckert knew somebody high up in the White House.

But after the reports of the pornographic pictures, the escort Web sites featuring nude pictures (all right, all right, he wore his combat boots, too), and his homosexuality hit the mainstream, Gannon was flushed from the White House and wiped from *Talon News*. Citizens and legislators still scratch their heads, wondering how it happened that an anti-gay president who claims to be securing our borders can have his pressroom penetrated by a guy with no background and no qualifications aside from the fact that he really, really liked the administration.

Suddenly friendless, and left to deal with his hypocrisy alone, Gannon will have plenty of time to concentrate on preparations for his testimony in front of the grand jury investigating the Plame incident (although Gannon has since denied having been subpoenaed).

Hey, if you need a scapegoat for a felony, why not offer up an out-of-work hooker turned shill with a public record for covering up and a private history of taking it all off?

## MORALITY SCORE

**Hourly rate: $200. Weekend rate: $1,200. Endorsing Bush's antigay legislation while sleeping with men for money: priceless.**

# Representative David Dreier

## (R·CALIFORNIA)

I will tell you, I'm voting for all the American people. That's what I'm doing. And I'm standing up for what I believe is right for everyone.

—*David Dreier, defending twenty-four years of antigay voting on Sirius Satellite's OutQ gay-interest radio station*

## His Remarkable Career

A self-proclaimed "Reaganaut," So-Cal Congressman David Dreier and his movie-star mentor went to Washington in 1980, surfing the wave of Republican Revolution I. Dreier came to office, according to his official biography, with a vision "promoting individual liberty." Unless, of course, that individual is gay.

As a young congressman for California's Twenty-sixth District, Dreier was an admirable conservative—fighting taxes and helping to make government smaller. Most notably, however, he was a rabid supporter of Reagan's anti-Communist policy initiatives in Central and South America, and elsewhere.

He built a reputation as a party man. When the Communists were defeated (or the guerrilla movements in Central America had defeated them for us), it was time to battle gays and Dreier was as hard-line against these sinners and defilers of marriage as he was against the dirty Reds.

In 1996, Dreier voted for Bob Barr's Defense of Marriage Act. The next year, he voted against the Hate Crimes Prevention Act. In 1998, Dreier voted against allowing gays and lesbians to adopt children. The Christian Coalition was salivating—Dreier was a heartthrob of the right, and he could do no wrong. He received a 92 percent rating from the organization. Dreier was a certified Conservative honey.

By 1999, this staunch supporter of many antigay laws had gathered enough favor to become chairman of the House Rules Committee. Now one of the most powerful men in the House, Dreier established a rep among committee members for total commitment to GOP policies. The Manchurian candidate of the conservative crowd, Dreier continued voting the party line, and then some: in 1999 he opposed the Employment Non-Discrimination Act, as he had in 1996, which would have put safeguards in place to prevent discrimination against gays in hiring practices. He also voted to allow federally funded charities to discriminate against gays in employment.

And, in 2004, Dreier voted for the Marriage Protection Act. Though over fifty and unmarried with no children, Dreier positioned himself as a "family values" Republican (don't they all?). In 2000, he pandered to Hispanic voters in his Los Angeles County district, using the slogan "Family values don't stop at the Rio Grande." They did, apparently, stop at Dreier's front door.

## His Personal Commitment

Although Dreier was long suspected of being a gay man and voting against his own interests from the safety of the closet, a former reporter for several newspapers in his district, Mark Cromer, says no one checked out the story because newspapers in Dreier's district were owned by Media News Group (Cromer's former employer) and took a strongly conservative editorial position. The news organization's CEO is a staunch Republican. There was, it seems, a "Don't Ask, Don't Tell" policy going on in California's Twenty-sixth District.

But then gay activist blogger Mike Rogers struck again, claiming that his motives for outing antigay politicians followed what he called the "Barney Frank outing rule." The openly gay congressman has insisted that outing is permissible only when the people in question wield their power or leadership to hurt gays or deny them basic human rights. With his history of antigay voting—a record that spanned twenty-four years—Dreier more than passed the Frank test.

So Rogers, bloggers from Rawstory.com, Larry Flynt, and *LA Weekly* went to work, investigating Dreier's past, finding sources, corroborating those sources, and discovering that Dreier had been living with a man named Brad Smith.

His chief of staff.

Sleeping at the boss's house has advantages. Smith enjoyed a salary of $156,000 per year—higher than any chief of staff in the House, and only $400 short of presidential pooper scooper Karl Rove's annual salary. The congressman and his high-dollar manservant also did some globetrotting together. In 2004, the congressional newspaper *Roll Call* reported that Dreier, who chaired the Rules Committee— a committee that has nothing to do with foreign policy— was among the top ten most well-traveled congressmen: Together, Dreier and Smith spent a total of forty-five days abroad from 2001 to 2004. The buddies traveled to vital political and economic American allies like Sri Lanka, Micronesia, and Iceland. A spokesman said Dreier was gathering information for amendments.

So much for small government.

After the news of Dreier's alleged secret life broke, the congressman refused to deny it. In the same Sirius Radio interview in which he defended his voting record as simply being votes his constituents would want him to cast— votes that denied health care to AIDS victims, votes that made same-sex marriage illegal and endorsed the view that homosexuality is immoral, votes that made gay adoption impossible in Washington, D.C., and votes that allowed discrimination against gays—journalist Michelangelo Signorile asked the congressman point blank if he was a heterosexual.

"I'm not going to talk about that issue," Dreier said.

There was one redeeming element of Dreier's twenty-four-year career, and that was his steadfast opposition to the Federal Marriage Amendment. But, far from touting "rights for individuals" as the reason for his opposition to the bill, Dreier instead sided with other strict-constructionist Republicans who, as a matter of principle, didn't want to alter the Constitution.

It was the one "principled" vote Dreier ever cast.

## MORALITY SCORE

**Years spent refusing to confirm or deny his sexual preference: twenty-four. Years spent voting for antigay legislation: twenty-four. Days spent abroad with the man he lives with (on the federal dime): forty-five.**

# Ken Mehlman

**Chairman of the
Republican National Committee**

The president is leading based on principle. His principles are reflective of his values and his values are compassionate and conservative.

*—2004 Bush campaign chair Ken Mehlman
quoted in the* Washington Blade, *May 28, 2004, repeatedly declining
to confirm or deny his heterosexuality*

## His Remarkable Career

Ken Mehlman is the most eligible bachelor in Washington. With his dreamy eyes, his shock of sandy-brown hair, his chiseled jaw line, and his willowy frame, he is the pinup of Young Future Republicans of America everywhere. Thirty-seven and unmarried, on the Capitol Hill meat market, Mehlman is USDA prime rib.

But the main question interested parties have been whispering for years is: *Is he or isn't he?*

A graduate of Harvard Law School, Ken Mehlman practiced law for three years before turning to politics. His first stop was at the campaign offices of Representative Lamar Smith, a Republican from Texas. Smith's voting record is as red as the blood spilled in the name of civil rights.

In 1995, Mehlman managed the campaign of Representative Kay Granger (R-Texas). The Harvard lawyer-cum-cowboy took Granger to the top—she won reelection and named Mehlman her chief of staff from 1996 to 1999. Her voting record was as puckered as Smith's, though she did score twice as high as he did on the ACLU's civil rights rating curve at a stunning 14 percent.

Mehlman's Texas cowboy fetish really hit its stride, though, in 2000, when Bush tapped him to become national field director for the Bush/Cheney ticket. Under the banner of "compassionate conservatism," Mehlman shamelessly sold out gays by promoting a "family and moral values" platform that was the most threadbare euphemism for antihomosexual legislation, something a surprising number of people in this country were salivating for.

After Bush was awarded the White House by the Supreme Court, Mehlman was rewarded for his wily evasion by being named White House political director, a post he held from 2001 to 2003. For a very short period of time, Mehlman's conscience peeked its head out and he began bringing gay Republican lobbies (called the Austin 12) into agenda discussions. Three years later, however, Bush would decree, with Mehlman's full support, that marriage was between a man and a woman and that "we ought to codify that one way or another, and we've got lawyers looking at the best way to do that."

In February 2004, Bush formally announced his intentions to amend the constitution and ban same-sex marriage. Much like Senator Strom Thurmond's segregationist rhetoric, Bush framed the issue as a matter of constitutional law rather than civil rights. And, despite the divorces and trysts of many party cohorts supporting the legislation, Bush stuck to the argument that marriage is the glue of civilization.

"After more than two centuries of American jurisprudence, and millennia of human experience, a few judges and local authorities are presuming to change the most fundamental institution of civilization. Their actions have created confusion on an issue that requires clarity," Bush said.

Ever dutiful, Mehlman stood by his man. As campaign manager of the Bush/Cheney 2004 ticket and overseer of one of the most divisive elections in history, an election that turned largely on same-sex marriage and the Right's vehement opposition to it, Mehlman helped Bush achieve a career milestone: a majority vote in a presidential election.

Oh, it's rainin' votes, hallelujah, it's rainin' votes!

Mehlman had become the life of the stodgy Republican party; with Bush's full support, Mehlman was elected chair of the Republican National Committee.

But then a strange thing happened on the way to the Republican National Convention.

## His Personal Commitment

In a just world, it wouldn't matter whether Ken Mehlman is gay or straight. And, in a just world, politicians who win elections by whipping their constituents into a frothy mess about pervasive immorality and hedonism would not be pervasively immoral and hedonistic themselves. But this isn't a just world, and because Mehlman is responsible for promoting or making possible legislation that denies basic rights to gays, then the question is a valid one—perhaps even a vital one.

In November 2004, industrious blogger Mike Rogers, the leading gay activist responsible for outing other "family values" Republicans, reported successful attempts by the Bush/Cheney campaign to suppress the Mehlman story during the GOP National Convention. The Mehlman story was this: the sexuality of thirty-seven-year-old unmarried political wunderkind was ambiguous.

"During the Republican Convention, I was about to run a piece about Ken Mehlman," Rogers wrote on his site, blog active.com. "While I was writing the piece, the two sources I was in contact with told me that they were called by unnamed press folks at the GOP and had decided to not go public with their story. Around the same time, two New York City newspapers were called by press folks at the Bush Campaign attempting to kill the Mehlman story. . . . It worked."

Though leaning on the press proved successful for the Bush administration, Mike Rogers kept up his coverage. On November 30, he reported multiple sources close to Mehlman had vouched for his homosexuality, including one who said that Mehlman had approached him on two occasions at a popular Washington, D.C., gay bar.

Soon, it seemed as if everyone—except the mainstream press and Mehlman himself, who refused to either confirm or deny—was talking about the guy's sexuality. It wasn't prurient interest, the kind of masturbatory fascination most have with the cover subjects of *Us Weekly* and *Star*.

Then, mainstream radio talk-show host Randi Rhodes mentioned Mehlman's seeming duality on her show. Rogers posted the transcript and the audio file of the show in question, in which Rhodes said,

> This is a huge country with a lot of different thoughts and a lot of different ways to worship and a lot of different ways not to worship, that's who we are, it's what—we're a big tent and apparently it's gonna be fabulously decorated 'cause Ken Mehlman is head of the Republican National Committee and [whisper] he's gay. So, ya know . . . they send out these bigoted, horrifying pamphlets: "Democrats want to do away with the Bible." And then their own Supreme

Court doesn't want to hear the case. Then they send out more horrifying things. About gays . . . anti . . . homophobic . . . horrible gay-bashing stuff—turns out the guys that were sending them: Gay!

This rumor, if true, would be of historic interest: A notably antigay administration with a gay campaign chairman. Beyond that, it would be an extravagant act of evasion—the kind of evasion that would likely result in painful legislation for gays, legislation designed to pacify those among us who would have us believe that gays are equivalent, to use Trent Lott's metaphor, to kleptomaniacs and sex addicts.

## MORALITY SCORE

**Stories quashed: two. Sources stifled: two. Number of people whose civil rights have been curtailed with the help of one Wily Evader: tens of millions.**

# Arthur J. Finkelstein
## Republican Strategist

## His Remarkable Career

In April 2005, the *New York Times* reported that Bill Clinton had, uncharacteristically, felt moved to step up to his wife's defense (he has long tried to stay out of the spotlight when it comes to Mrs. Clinton's political career) over news that a well-known Republican strategist had begun to organize a PAC called Stop Her Now, aimed at thwarting Mrs. Clinton's reelection campaign in 2006.

"I was sort of sad when I read it," the former president said.

Why the long face, Bill? It turns out that the man behind the plan of attack was Arthur J. Finkelstein, architect of Jesse Helms's notorious 1990 reelection campaign, which was roundly derided for its reliance on homophobia to win votes, and adviser to several antigay politicians, including gay-marriage-phobic governors Mitt Romney of Massachusetts and George Pataki of New York. Finkelstein hoped to mimic the ad campaign run by Swift Boat Veterans for Truth, which devastated John Kerry's presidential campaign.

New York native Fink has long been a figure deeply involved in extreme right-wing politics: he helped keep Helms legislating after helping the old man launch a major come-from-behind 1990 victory by mobilizing voters with antigay rhetoric (Helms has called homosexuals "disgusting"). In addition to his work with governors Romney and Pataki, Fink also worked for former Israeli Prime Minister Benjamin Netanyahu in his 1999 campaign to defeat Ehud Barak. In political circles, Fink is known as either a political genius or a whirling dervish of hate and negativity. A near recluse, Fink rarely grants interviews. There's a good reason for that.

## His Personal Commitment

In December 2004, a small, quiet ceremony took place at a home in Ipswich, Massachusetts. In attendance were two men—partners for nearly forty years—as well as a gay state official, who presided over the civil ceremony, relatives of the couple, and a state legislator. The couple was married so that, one of the men said, they could ensure that they had the same benefits as those available to heterosexual couples.

"I believe that visitation rights, health-care benefits, and other human relationship contracts that are taken for granted by all married people should be available to partners," the man said.

The man was Arthur J. Finkelstein. The same Arthur J. Finkelstein who engineered a homophobic election campaign for a Southern bigot. The same Arthur J. Finkelstein who is a close adviser to two governors who refuse to recognize same-sex marriage. The same Arthur J. Finkelstein who wants to destroy Hillary Clinton in the 2006 New York Senate campaign.

"Either this guy believes his party is not serious and he's totally Machiavellian," Bill Clinton said, "or he may be blinded by self-loathing." Rather than explain his logic, Fink has kept mum, relying on others to do his dirty work for him. Michael McKeon, another Republican strategist and a Pataki aide, told the *Times* that he was shocked at Clinton's comments.

"It's really beneath a former president to comment on someone's personal life like that. After everything he has been through in his own life, you'd think he'd know better."

Fink had been outed by *Boston* magazine in 1996, but continued his biting attacks against Democratic politicians and causes. Despite the avalanche of criticism he has faced from gay activists for what just might be construed as hypocrisy, Fink has honed his pro–right wing messages and is widely credited for making the very word "liberal" a vicious accusation.

MORALITY SCORE

Homophobic campaigns engineered: one. Anti–gay marriage governors advised: two. Anti-Democratic PACs formed: one. Same-sex marriages: one.

# Dr. Paul Crouch

**Trinity Broadcasting Network Godhead**

## His Remarkable Career

Dr. Paul Crouch believes in many things. Among them, that Christians are "little gods"; that Jesus did not pay for our sins on the cross, but in the fires of hell; that we can "command God by our words"; and that poverty and illness are the result of being a bad Christian. Oh, and that you are a good Christian only if you shell out some cash to keep TBN (and Dr. Paul Crouch) afloat.

"Pastor Paul Crouch looked into the camera and told his flock that Trinity Broadcasting Network needed eight million dollars to spread the Gospel through India and save one billion souls from damnation," the *LA Times* reported in 2004. "Crouch said even viewers who couldn't afford a $1,000 pledge should take a 'step of faith' and make one anyway. The Lord would repay them many times over, he said. 'Do you think God would have any trouble getting a thousand dollars extra to you somehow?' he asked during a 'Praise-a-thon' broadcast from Trinity's studios in Costa Mesa."

And if you dare hold off on sending that check in because you've got bills to pay or babies to feed, beware: "If you have been healed or saved or blessed through TBN and have not contributed . . . you are robbing God and will lose your reward in heaven."

From God's lips to your ears.

Trinity Broadcasting Network, or TBN, is the cable station that you flip past, thinking it beamed from somebody's basement studio in Dubuque. Suited gents swap deliverance for dollars, and dignity for heavily pomaded hairdos. From Arthur Blessitt to Creflo A. Dollar and his wife, Taffi, if you hate same-sex marriage as much as you love getting old folks to fork over their retirement money, you've probably preached on TBN.

Dr. Paul Crouch is the brains behind TBN. We'll call him Dr. Eyebrows. And that plastic lady under the blond hair next to him? That's Jan Crouch, his wife. We'll call her Mrs. Teeth.

You might be asking yourself right about now: God, will they ever learn? One would think after the scandals of Jim Bakker, Jimmy Swaggart, and countless other false prophets of prime-time TV, people would keep their wallets safely tucked into a pocket. But in 2003, TBN reported $197 million in gross revenues. Crouch's satellite networks span heaven, delivering dogma and collecting money—with the tenacity of a repo man—whenever they touch earth.

Unlike his hero, Jesus, Dr. Eyebrows is a filthy rich white Protestant. The *LA Times* reported in September 2004 that the company Crouch founded paid Crouch and his wife salaries that totaled nearly a million dollars a year. Jesus crossed the desert in sandals. Dr. Eyebrows trots the globe in a $7.2 million Canadair turbojet.

## His Personal Commitment

In 1997, when he wasn't providing airtime to the antigay, antiabortion, antiscience, pro-money scene, Dr. Eyebrows busily hushed up allegations of a gay love affair.

Former TBN employee Enoch Lonnie Ford filed a wrongful termination suit against the company, claiming he'd been fired after a gay love affair with Crouch. Ford reportedly demanded a whopping $10 million to effectively stop him from publishing an exposé of his affair with Crouch. What would Jesus do? Probably take the high road, pray for this poor sinner, and turn the other cheek. What did Dr. Eyebrows do? He had his network call Ford a crackhead: "The accuser is a convicted felon and longtime drug abuser who has been imprisoned for years for serious crimes ranging from child sexual molestation to using illegal drugs such as crack cocaine. . . . It is a reprehensible fact of modern life that public persons like Dr. Crouch are targets of such dishonest, false and scandalous claims."

Why TBN kept rehiring a man who committed multiple felonies is a topic for another day. Obviously, Ford was a charlatan looking for a quick payoff from the very man who founded the family values network. That must be why Crouch's son told the *LA Times*, "I am devastated; I am confronted with having to face the fact that my father is a homosexual."

Dr. Eyebrows, ever the man of faith, promptly paid Ford $425,000 before he, God, and a jury had the chance to reveal the true sinner in open court. The agreement included a hush provision on Ford, so he couldn't scare the flock with tales of Crouch's frolic.

Dr. Eyebrows maintains control of his ever-growing network, and continues to wish hell and damnation upon his critics. TBN added ten million viewers or rather, "souls" as they call them, in the Philadelphia/New Jersey market. Mrs. Teeth has started a new program for children in Haiti, who could probably dine for a decade on her quarterly hairspray budget.

## MORALITY SCORE

**TV stations delivering traditional values: 6,525. Satellites: forty-seven. Jilted gay lovers: one.**

# Dan Gurley and Jay Banning

**Bush Campaign Architects, Hatemongers, Gay Men**

There is a line drawn in America today. On one side are the radicals trying to uproot our traditional values and our culture. They're fighting to hijack the institution of marriage, plotting to legalize partial-birth abortion, and working to take God out of the pledge of allegiance and force the worst of Hollywood on the rest of America.

*— Radio ad sponsored by the Republican National Committee whose field directors are Dan Gurley and Jay Banning*

## Their Remarkable Careers

In 2004, George W. Bush's reelection campaign team leaned so far to the right they almost toppled and crushed Rick Santorum. As Bush's campaign staff would have it, their man George was antigay, antiabortion, anti–free speech, pro-war and (by some strange measure for a fellow who was pro-war) pro-God. This carefully cultivated image was the result of years of antigay, antiabortion, anti–free speech, and pro-war maneuverings (we'd hesitate to call any of the Bush initiatives "pro-God"—we'll let the Big Guy sort that out for himself), but it was also the crowning achievement of two brilliant members of Bush's campaign staff. A couple of gay guys.

Republican National Committee Field Director Dan Gurley and Chief Financial Officer Jay Banning orchestrated and supervised one the most hate-infected propaganda campaigns in the last fifty years, including a platform that was proudly antigay. Well done, boys.

Jay Banning became the Republican National Committee's CFO during Reagan's first term. More than twenty years later, he helped raise and administer $270 million for the RNC.

Dan Gurley was picked as the RNC's pivot man in the 2004 election cycle for the presidential election, as well as for select senatorial and congressional campaigns.

Both men were good at their jobs—shoring up firm majorities in Congress and winning a second term for a president who had never won his first. How did they do it? Hate-mongering, folks. Hatemongering.

In the most famous instance, Gurley, Banning and Co. mailed homophobic flyers to select Southern states. One mailer circulated in Arkansas featured a photo of the Bible with the word "BANNED" written over it, next to a picture of a man putting a ring on another man's finger. A caption reads "This will be Arkansas if you don't vote."

The flyer went on to explain, "Our traditional values are under assault by Liberal politicians and their hand-picked activist judges. They are using the courts to impose their radical agenda."

At the GOP convention, the Gurleymen were at it again. This time, they were institutionalizing homophobia in the Republican platform: "We strongly support President Bush's call for a Constitutional amendment that fully protects marriage, and we believe that neither federal nor state judges nor bureaucrats should force states to recognize other living arrangements as equivalent to marriage."

## Their Personal Commitments

Despite their fervent support of their boss, Gurley and Banning give a whole new meaning to "playing for the other team."

As Dan Gurley supervised the production of pamphlets that condemned same-sex couples, he busily attempted to couple with the same sex. His profile on Gay.com (with accompanying photographs) read: "Sexuality: gay; looking for: men; interested in: action/sex." His profile went on to detail his desire for unprotected sex, his enjoyment of politics and the military lifestyle (maybe we should hook him up with

Jeff Gannon), and concluded " . . . in many ways I am my own scene."

Who knew that self-loathing hypocrites impeding the social progress of peers could be their own "scenes"?

After deleting his profile, Gurley admitted to blog active.com that he was gay.

Jay Banning was yet another target of Mike Rogers's investigative efforts, and also admitted that he was gay. When asked whether his sexuality posed a problem in his profession, Banning said, "Uh, we don't discuss it," and added that he didn't believe being gay was a problem at his workplace, Homophobe Central.

The Bush campaign and the RNC have routinely refused to publicize the number of openly gay men working in their antigay offices, but the chilling fact is that the two lead architects of George W. Bush's 2004 reelection campaign—leading to the most homophobic administration in recent memory—are gay, as is the chairman (the *chairman*) of the Republican National Committee. With friends like these . . .

MORALITY SCORE

**Seedy online profiles: one. Open admissions: two. Money raised for antigay movement: $270 million. Number of gays working in the RNC: undisclosed.**

# (Dis) Honorable
## Mentions

> What you do speaks so loud that I cannot
> hear what you say.
>
> —*Ralph Waldo Emerson*

WHILE NOT EVERYONE CAN BE a general in the battle to sanctify marriage, everyone has the potential to sign up and contribute, one sex scandal at a time. Not loud (or obnoxious) enough to be considered blowhards, too powerless to be members of the Silent Majority, and lacking the red-hot duplicity of the Self-Loathers, these minions of marriage are not as visible as those already profiled. They are our (Dis)Honorable Mentions, and we are thankful for their fortitude in the fight to keep prayer in school and gays out of wedlock. Bob Dole might not have won the presidency but he can still sport Viagra-assisted wood for Britney Spears. What's more American than that?

Well, some graying hippies might say "democracy" or "equal opportunity." Don't believe it—for the last thirty years, the Republicans have been painstakingly erasing these concepts from our collective concept of America, replacing them with a vision of a country in which everyone is straight, well-armed, oversexed (but quiet about it), drugged up (but only on prescription pain pills), drunk off their asses in Beltway bars, and ready to bomb poor brown people in faraway countries.

As they say, it takes a village.

. . .

### Jack Ryan
### Former Republican Candidate for Senate (Illinois)
*Silent Majority*

In the spring of 2004, ultraconservative hottie Jack Ryan announced he was withdrawing from the Illinois U.S. Senate race, leaving Alan Keyes and Barack Obama to duke it out. Why would an anti–same sex marriage, pro–family values Republican candidate abandon his candidacy in the middle of an election?

By now, do you really have to ask?

Jack Ryan ran his election on a family values, anti–same sex marriage platform. Ryan said, with a straight face, that "marriage can only be defined as that union between one man and one woman," despite the fact that he knew that sealed away in divorce papers was a very interesting narrative about his desire to unionize with his television star wife, Jeri, in front of other unions.

When divorce proceedings between the forty-four-year-old former investment banker and his beautiful blond wife, Jeri (she starred as a Borg on *Star Trek: Voyager*), were unsealed, a picture of a sanctified union emerged that included sex clubs, whips and chains, cages, and group sex. According to Jeri, Ryan took her to sex clubs in various cities and asked her to have sex with him in front of other patrons. At the sex club in Paris where Ryan pleaded his case to his wife, Jeri said, "People were having sex everywhere. I cried. I was physically ill. He became very upset with me and said it was not a 'turn on' for me to cry."

When the allegations became public, the devout Catholic vowed to stand strong and not give up his candidacy. But as his Republican buddies stopped returning his phone calls, Ryan read the writing on the wall and finally announced he would not seek office.

While the media had a field day with the more salacious details of Ryan's downfall, what went uncommented upon was the troubling disparity between the standards of marriage Ryan would have legislated for American citizens and the standards he himself upheld. No one would dispute Ryan's right to participate in consensual sex with his wife, no matter how kinky—it was just harder to swallow coming from a guy who wanted to dispute the rights of other Americans to participate in consensual sex.

### Senator Bob Dole
### (R-Kansas, Retired)
*Silent Majority*

Some years back, Bob Dole began hawking Viagra. The commercial, with its slow dissolves, its shots of Dole looking out windows longingly, of Dole smiling and looking away from the camera demurely, promised millions of men the ability to get the old guy working again, and who better to serve as spokesman than the old guy himself, Bob Dole. It requires some imagination, then, to recall that Bob Dole was perhaps one of the most influential Republican leaders in American politics during the twentieth century. The longtime senator from Russell, Kansas, served as Republican National Committee chairman, Senate Republican leader, GOP precinct captain, and, of course, presidential nominee.

Dole has famously summed up his priorities this way: "God, honor, country, family." On the campaign trail and in televised debates, he has lamented America's move away from "Judeo-Christian family values." He called Clinton a "philistine" and, along with Newt Gingrich, launched the most excoriating attacks against the former president in the wake of the Lewinsky scandal.

And yet, for all his huffin' and puffin', Dole's own track record when it comes to marriage is spotty, to say the least. While married to wife Phyllis, Dole reportedly engaged in dalliances with a number of flight attendants and one woman named Elizabeth. Dole's only child, Robin, was born during the marriage to Phyllis, but in 1972, Dole left his wife. For a good part of his legislative career, many voters didn't even know Dole had a child—he himself was quoted as saying, "I don't think I really knew [Robin] well. I was there for ceremonial things in school, but mostly they [Phyllis and Robin] were here and I was not." Bob Dole chose divorce. During the last year of their marriage, Phyllis has said, Dole was home for dinner on only four occasions.

### Senator Jim Bunn
### (R-Oregon, Retired)
*Blowhard*

With the strong support of the Christian Coalition, hyperconservative Jim Bunn won his Senate seat running on a platform of strict morality and Christian values. But there's something in the water in Washington, because, shortly after arriving at Capitol Hill, Bunn dumped his wife of seventeen years and the mother of his five children, and took up with a young aide, later marrying her. He promoted his new bride to chief of staff, making her the nation's highest paid congressional aide. Bunn's constituents elected not to elect him again, and he is currently a jailer for Yamhill County, Oregon.

### Representative Mark Foley
### (R-Florida)
*Wily Evader*

Representative Mark Foley, a fifty-year-old bachelor from West Palm Beach, Florida, is "revolted" by rumors that he is a homosexual. In fact, the good Republican Christian from Florida's Sixteenth Congressional District says they are downright "unforgivable." Among the unforgiven: *Salon,* the *Fort Lauderdale Sun-Sentinel, St. Petersburg Times, The Advocate, Miami Herald,* and countless political blogs that have raised the issue of the congressman's sexuality in the context of his support of the Defense of Marriage Act. In fact, some political observers call the congressman's homosexuality an "open secret" in Washington.

"In interviews for this story," a reporter for *The Advocate* wrote during Foley's first run for Congress in 1994, "several people close to the forty-one-year-old from West Palm Beach described him as a gay man, although one said he dated women." Foley's response? To blame the Democratic party (an accusation that strains credulity when you consider that, prior to Foley's response to the rumors, almost everyone who mentioned the issue to the *St. Petersburg Times,* at least, was Republican).

"Frankly, I don't think what kind of personal relationships I have in my private life is of any relevance to anyone else," Foley said.

We agree. The problem is the Republican Party's continuing fascination with the private lives of others, and its attempt to legislate its bogus morality based on its interpretation of morality.

In 2003, Foley called a preemptive press conference to deny the reports that he is gay. "He wanted reporters to know that he won't answer questions about his sexuality," Adam C. Smith of the *St. Petersburg Times* wrote. "Don't ask, won't tell."

Florida State Senator Stephen Wise, for one, didn't believe the rumors about Foley: "I think the standards of family values are pretty strong in the Republican Party," Wise said with a straight face. "The issue is we're looking for candidates who have good family values and care about the family."

While Mark Foley's voting record is remarkably "pro-gay" (speaking in relative terms—he supports non-discrimination legislation, for example), his silence in the face of attacks against gays, like those spewed by Rick Santorum on the floor of Congress, also makes him a member of the Silent Majority. What is "revolting and unforgivable" is Foley's weak attempt to make himself more appealing to Florida's right-wing voters by calling any suggestion that he's gay "revolting and unforgivable."

Foley has wished aloud that politicians were judged by their track records and job performance rather than their personal lives—and yet that wish seemed not to extend to President Clinton when Foley voted to impeach the beleaguered politician with a good "track record" and an excellent "job performance."

### Senator Tim Hutchinson
### (R-Arkansas, Retired)
*Blowhard*

In 1999, conservative Republican Tim Hutchinson was on top of the world. He was a rising star in the U.S. Congress, and one half of a Republican dynasty in the making (his brother is Asa Hutchinson). The Arkansas senator was, like so many of his Republican counterparts, concerned about the fragile state of the American family, an institution that seemed headed for collapse if right wingers didn't step in and take it back from divorcées, the gays, and other knuckleheads. The Republicans loved him.

Well, not all of them. In a curious scene of cannibalism, the *Arkansas Review*—a conservative political publication—revealed that Hutch was about to file for a divorce from his wife of twenty-nine years (and the mother of his three children). The lucky replacement wife? Thirty-one-year-old Randi Fredholm, a former Hutch aide, with whom he had allegedly been carrying on an affair for some time.

Hutch, a Southern Baptist minister who had voted to impeach Clinton, had been a fervent family values man—it had been a major point of his election campaigns.

"And while we're troubled by this sad news," the editors at the *Arkansas Review* wrote, "Tim Hutchinson's office and his support of family values make this a news story." The editor and owner of the *Review*, Sam Sellers, had managed Hutch's first campaign for Congress, and the senator had not only served as Sellers's premarital counselor during the months leading up to the editor's marriage, he also married Sellers and his wife.

When the news broke, Hutch kept mum, but a few months later, he married Randi Fredholm.

### Representative Ken Calvert
### (R-California)
*Blowhard*

Voted yes to a constitutional amendment banning same-sex marriage.

Voted yes to banning gay adoptions.

Voted yes to an impeachment of a standing president for engaging in infidelity in the White House.

Elected to solicit the services of a prostitute in 1993.

Such are the highlights of the career of Ken Calvert, the far-right-wing Republican representative from California's Forty-third Congressional District. With a 100 percent approval rating from the Christian Coalition (and a 7 percent rating from the ACLU), Ken Calvert positioned himself as a defender of marriage and of families. During impeachment proceedings, Calvert said, "We can't forgive what occurred between the president and Lewinsky."

And yet this moral model had, just a few years before, been caught in an unforgivable position himself—in his car with a prostitute's face in his lap. Around Thanksgiving on November 28, the congressman drove to Corona, California. Two policemen happened upon Calvert's car and, according to a police report that was sealed for more than a year while Calvert denied the whole incident, saw the following:

> I observed a male subject in the driver seat. . . . As I made my way to the driver door, a female immediately sat up straight in the front passenger seat. It appeared as if her head was originally laying in the driver's lap. . . . I noticed that the male subject was placing his penis into his unzipped dress slacks, and was trying to hide it with his untucked shirt. . . . The male subject started his vehicle and placed it into drive and proceeded to leave. I ordered him three times to turn off the vehicle, and he finally stopped and complied. . . . The male identified himself as Kenneth Stanton Calvert [Republican who represents California's Forty-third Congressional District].

After more than a year of vehement denials, Calvert finally admitted to the hummer, offering the excuse: "I was feeling intensely lonely." It was an excuse Calvert would have accepted from no other disgraced politician but himself.


### Randal David Ankeney
### Former GOP Rising Star
*Silent Majority*


Randy Randal rose fast in the ranks of the Colorado GOP, no mean feat for a modern culture warrior (Colorado being the home of both congressional sponsors of the Federal Marriage Amendment). An attorney well known in state political circles for his campaign volunteerism, Ankeney was one of those annoying Republicans who name their dogs after disgraced Republican presidents (Nixon, in his case). The *Rocky Mountain News* called him a "fixture in El Paso County Republican politics." By age thirty, Ankeney pulled down $63,000 per year on the public payroll as Colorado Republican Governor Bill Owens's appointee to the Colorado Springs branch of the state economic development board.

So far, so good.

But then this darling of perhaps the most conservative state Republican party in the country was tossed in the clink for having sex with underage girls. Way underage. In 2001, the thirty-year-old Ankeney met a thirteen-year-old girl in an

Internet chat room. She agreed to meet him. Once he got her in his clutches at his home, prosecutors said, Ankeney got her drunk, smoked her out with marijuana, photographed her without her top, and raped her. When he was finished, he dropped the child off at a fast-food restaurant, where she called a relative, who called the cops.

Once the allegations against Ankeney became public, a second girl, a seventeen-year-old former co-worker from a election campaign, came forward, charging that Ankeney had raped her as well.

Ankeney pleaded guilty but tried to change his mind before he was sentenced. The court didn't let him, and gave him a new kind of governmental appointment to the tune of twenty-two years.

### Parker J. Bena
### Former Republican Elector (Virginia)
*Silent Majority*

Republican Elector Parker J. Bena's favorite movie is *The Ten Commandments*. His second favorite movie is that violent orgy of men and horses, *Ben-Hur*. How do we know this? Bena typed up his Top Ten Favorite Movies list at Listmania. com. Bena, it seems, spent a lot of time online talking about movies—but movies weren't the only things that captured his online interest.

Described by various newspapers in the aftermath of his downfall as a "Republican activist," Bena was one of Virginia's thirteen Republican electors in 2000. If being dedicated to God, country, the preservation of morality, and all those other Republican requirements is a crime, then Bena wanted to be locked up. And he was, but not for professing allegiance to the Republican party. He was convicted of possessing kiddie porn.

Bena told the FBI about an unsolicited e-mail in his inbox that contained images of children performing sexual acts—but after investigating, the FBI discovered that Bena himself had downloaded the images. Bena pleaded guilty to possession of child pornography, a federal offense, and received a thirty-month sentence in federal prison.

In his defense, there is no commandment reading, "Thou shall not look at naked toddlers."

### Representative Jim Kolbe
### (R-Arizona)
*Self-Loather*

It's okay to be Republican. It's okay to be gay. But it's hypocrisy to be a gay Republican passing antigay legislation. And yet—that's what Representative Jim Kolbe did. In 1996, Kolbe voted yes to pass the Defense of Marriage Act—legislation drafted for the "moral majority" by two-time divorcé and hedonist at large Bob Barr in order to defend marriage from people like Jim Kolbe. This vote was cast the same year Kolbe was forced to come out and admit he was, in the words of former New Jersey Governor Jim McGreevey, a gay American. Continuing his pattern of self-hatred, in 2000, Kolbe endorsed Bush Jr. and the goals of the GOP by addressing the Republican National Convention on trade issues. The Texas delegation underscored their state's traditional respect for diversity by keeping their heads bowed throughout Kolbe's speech, as if to imply that they were praying for his safe passage straight to hell.

Though Kolbe never discussed gay rights in his 2000 convention speech, he thought he was taking a stand for gay rights. He told ABC's Sam Donaldson that his speech "does make a statement to the Republican Party and, I think, to the convention."

Four years after helping Bush "win" the 2000 election, and after a marked improvement in his own voting record in regards to gay rights, Kolbe found himself battling an amendment to the U.S. Constitution that would deny him a basic right. Kolbe was not invited to speak at the 2004 GOP Convention. It wasn't his stance on NAFTA that turned the party off.

# The Defense of Marriage Act

---

ONE HUNDRED FOURTH CONGRESS

*of the*

UNITED STATES OF AMERICA
AT THE SECOND SESSION

---

Begun and held at the City of Washington on Wednesday, the third day of January, one thousand nine hundred and ninety-six

AN ACT

To define and protect the institution of marriage.

*Be it enacted by the Senate and House of Representatives of the United States of America in Congress assembled,*

## SECTION 1. SHORT TITLE.

This Act may be cited as the "Defense of Marriage Act."

## SEC. 2. POWERS RESERVED TO THE STATES.

(a) IN GENERAL—Chapter 115 of title 28, United States Code, is amended by adding after section 1738B the following:

## SEC. 1738C. CERTAIN ACTS, RECORDS, AND PROCEEDINGS AND THE EFFECT THEREOF

No State, territory, or possession of the United States, or Indian tribe, shall be required to give effect to any public act, record, or judicial proceeding of any other State, territory, possession, or tribe respecting a relationship between persons of the same sex that is treated as a marriage under the laws of such other State, territory, possession, or tribe, or a right or claim arising from such relationship.

(b) CLERICAL AMENDMENT—The table of sections at the beginning of chapter 115 of title 28, United States Code, is amended by inserting after the item relating to section 1738B the following new item:

1738C. Certain acts, records, and proceedings and the effect thereof.

## SEC. 3. DEFINITION OF MARRIAGE.

(a) IN GENERAL—Chapter 1 of title 1, United States Code, is amended by adding at the end the following:

## SEC. 7. DEFINITION OF "MARRIAGE" AND "SPOUSE"

In determining the meaning of any Act of Congress, or of any ruling, regulation, or interpretation of the various administrative bureaus and agencies of the United States, the word "marriage" means only a legal union between one man and one woman as husband and wife, and the word "spouse" refers only to a person of the opposite sex who is a husband or a wife.

(b) CLERICAL AMENDMENT—The table of sections at the beginning of chapter 1 of title 1, United States Code, is amended by inserting after the item relating to section 6 the following new item:

7. Definition of "marriage" and "spouse."

*Speaker of the House of Representatives.*
*Vice President of the United States and*
*President of the Senate.*

# The Federal Marriage Amendment

## 108TH CONGRESS
### 1ST SESSION

## H. J. RES. 56

Proposing an amendment to the Constitution of the United States relating to marriage.

**IN THE HOUSE OF REPRESENTATIVES**

**MAY 21, 2003**

Mrs. MUSGRAVE (for herself, Mr. HALL, Mr. MCINTYRE, Mr. PETERSON of Minnesota, Mrs. JO ANN DAVIS of Virginia, and Mr. VITTER) introduced the following joint resolution; which was referred to the Committee on the Judiciary

---

**JOINT RESOLUTION**

Proposing an amendment to the Constitution of the United States relating to marriage.

*Resolved by the Senate and House of Representatives of the United States of America in Congress assembled (two-thirds of each House concurring therein),* That the following article is proposed as an amendment to the Constitution of the United States, which shall be valid to all intents and purposes as part of the Constitution when ratified by the legislatures of three-fourths of the several States within seven years after the date of its submission for ratification:

ARTICLE—

SECTION 1. Marriage in the United States shall consist only of the union of a man and a woman. Neither this Constitution or the constitution of any State, nor state or federal law, shall be construed to require that marital status or the legal incidents thereof be conferred upon unmarried couples or groups.

# SOURCES

Whenever possible, Web addresses have been posted along with the article cited. Web articles with no posted date have been cited with the date author accessed the information on the site.

## INTRODUCTION

. . . *only purpose of marriage is procreation:* Dahlia Lithwick, "Holy Matrimony: What's Really Undermining the Sanctity of Marriage," *Slate,* November 20, 2003, www.slate.com/id/2091475.

*There's no question that the effort to protect marriage:* Kathleen Rutledge, "Dobson on the Gay Marriage Battle," *Christianity Today,* December 30, 2004, www.christianitytoday.com/ct/2005/001/21.60.html.

## BLOWHARDS

### Representative Bob Barr

*The very foundations of our society:* Bob Barr, *Congressional Record,* 104th Congress, July 12, 1996.

*Bob Barr represented the Seventh District:* "About Bob Barr," www.bobbarr.org (accessed April 15, 2005).

*Champion of the National Rifle Association:* Robert Dreyfuss, "Uzi Does It," *Mother Jones,* September/October 1996, www.motherjones.com/news/feature/1996/09/barr.html.

. . . *and been sued for child support:* David Plotz, "Rep. Bob Barr, He Shouts What His Fellow Republicans Won't Even Whisper:

Impeach Clinton!" *Slate*, February 22, 1998, http://slate.msn.com/id/1853.

. . . *by licking whipped cream from the cleavages:* Lloyd Grove, "Rep. Barr's New Quest: Impeachment," *Washington Post*, February 10, 1998, www.washingtonpost.com/wp-srv/politics/special/clinton/stories/barr021098.htm.

. . . *Barr said it had been done for charitable reasons:* Andrew Phillips, "Clinton Parries Sexual Allegations," *MacLean's* (Canada), March 30, 1998, http://tceplus.com/indexcfm?PgNm=TCE&Params=M1ARTM00111567; Scott Henry, "Right-Wing Smackdown," *Creative Loafing Atlanta,* July 24, 2002, http://atlanta.creativeloafing.com/2002-07-24/cover_news.html.

*As a leading torch bearer in the Clinton lynch mob:* Plotz, "Rep. Bob Barr."

. . . *Barr became a target of* Hustler *publisher:* "Publisher Larry Flynt Levels Accusations at Rep. Bob Barr," CNN, January 12, 1999, www.cnn.com/ALLPOLITICS/stories/1999/01/12/flynt.01/.

*In an affidavit to* Hustler, *Barr's second wife, Gail, a former CIA analyst, said Barr consented to and paid for her 1983 abortion. She later came to realize:* Gail Barr, "Gail Barr's Affidavit to *Hustler* Magazine," as reprinted by *American Politics Journal,* January 19, 1999, www.americanpolitics.com.

. . . *the righteous congressman would not dignify the accusations with a comment:* Robert Scheer, "Flynt Hustles Tale of GOP Hypocrisy, Impeachment: Publisher's Revelations Bring into Question Whether Rep. Barr Can Claim the Moral High Ground," *Los Angeles Times,* January 19, 1999, home edition, p. 7.

*Yet in Gail Barr's affidavit:* Barr, "Gail Barr's Affidavit," and J. R. Moehringer, "Rep. Barr Inspires Loyalty, Loathing in Home District," *Los Angeles Times,* January 19, 1999, home edition, p. 15.

## Representative Newt Gingrich

*In 1943, an unmarried Pennsylvania teenager:* Peter J. Boyer, "The Long March of Newt Gingrich," *Frontline,* PBS, January 1996, www.pbs.org/wgbh/pages/frontline/newt/newtchron.html.

*Always the teacher's pet:* Boyer, "Long March of Newt Gingrich."

*"We had oral sex":* Gail Sheehy, "The Inner Quest of Newt Gingrich," *Vanity Fair,* September 1995.

*... "The Newt Defense":* Stephen Talbot, "Newt's Glass House," *Salon,* August 28, 1998, www.salon.com/news/1998/08/28news. html.

*In 1981, as she was receiving cancer treatment:* David Osborne, "Newt Gingrich: Shining Knight of the Post-Reagan Right," *Mother Jones,* November 1, 1984, www.motherjones.com/news/feature/1984/11/osborne.html.

*The girl on the Hill was:* Andy Soltis, "Newt's Fooling Around with His Girl on the Hill," *New York Post,* August 12, 1999, p. 8; and Timothy Burger and Owen Moritz, "Newt Plays House with New Squeeze," *New York Daily News,* August 12, 1999.

*"Woody Allen family values":* Tim Graham, "Democrats' Woody Allen Family Values," *Media Reality Check,* vol. 2, no. 11, March 12, 1998, www.mediaresearch.org/realitycheck/1998/fax19980312. asp; and *The Progressive Review,* April 2004, http://prorev.com/gaywed.htm.

*... Federal Election Commission charged him for receiving illegal campaign contributions:* Michael Duffy, "Back to the Bench," *Time,* December 11, 1995, www.time.com/time/archive/preview/0,10987,983827,00.html.

*Three tabloids exposed Gingrich's six-year affair with Bisek:* Soltis, "Newt's Fooling Around"; Burger and Moritz, "Newt Plays House"; and David Corn, "The Big One That Got Away," *Salon,* August 12, 1999, http://archive.salon.com/news/feature/1999/08/12/gingrich/.

SOURCES 175

"*. . . So all I'll say is that I've led a human life*": Patricia Mays, "Gingrich Wife Can Question Woman," *Associated Press,* August 13, 1999.

*. . . so Gingrich resigned in January 1999:* Ann Curley, David Ensor, Bob Franken, and John King, "Gingrich Calls It Quits," CNN, November 6, 1998, www.cnn.com/ALLPOLITICS/stories/1998/11/06/gingrich.

*. . . legislators who bounce checks:* Boyer, "Long March of Newt Gingrich."

*Ann Coulter*

*. . . Earth is yours. Take it. Rape it:* "The Wisdom of Ann Coulter," *Washington Monthly,* October 2001, www.washingtonmonthly.com/features/2001/0111.coulterwisdom.html; and Eric Alterman, "Devil in a Blue Dress," *The Nation,* September 23, 2002, www.thenation.com/doc.mhtml?i=20020923&s=alterman.

*. . . Coulter was a smart chick:* Anncoulter.org, www.anncoulter.org/bio.html (accessed April 26, 2005).

*Her inane and tedious drivel:* "The Wisdom of Ann Coulter," and Alterman, "Devil in a Blue Dress."

*. . . described Harriman as a woman who had slept her way to the top:* Howard Kurtz, "The Blonde Flinging Bombshells at Clinton," *Washington Post,* October 16, 1998, final edition, p. D1.

*. . . "We should invade their countries, kill their leaders, and convert them to Christianity:* James Meek, "Invade Their Countries, Kill Their Leaders, and Convert Them to Christianity," *The Guardian,* September 24, 2004, http://film.guardian.co.uk/features/featurepages/0,4120,1311287,00.html; and Ann Coulter, "This Is War," *National Review,* September 13, 2001, www.nationalreview.com/coulter.shtml/.

*Her expertise is enhanced by her rich dating history:* NNDB.com, www.nndb.com/people/474/000022408/ (accessed April 26, 2005).

*Gary Bauer*

*After dodging the Vietnam draft:* "Gary Bauer, a Chat with a Presidential Candidate," CNN, May 13, 1999, www.cnn.com/chat/transcripts/bauer.html.

*He served in the Reagan administration for eight years:* "Gary Bauer," Ambassador Speakers Bureau and Literary Agency, http://garybauer.ambassadoragency.com/client_profile.cfm/cid/161?categories_id=6.

. . . *"a small cadre of cultural revolutionaries, militant homosexuals:* Family Research Council, direct mailing, October 1990.

. . . *stances on homosexuality that could politely be termed "anti-gay":* Richard L. Berke, "Flurry of Anti-Gay Remarks as GOP Fearing Backlash," *New York Times,* June 30, 1998; and Gary L. Bauer, "Questions and Answers on Homosexuality," April 13, 1998, at Harvard University, document included with Family Research Council direct mailing, May 8, 1998, www.barf.org/archive/family_research_council/bauer-harvard-questions.html.

*"Adultery is a big deal":* "Gary Bauer's Skeleton Closet," Real People for Real Change, www.realchange.org/bauer.htm (accessed April 26, 2005).

. . . *nine of his senior staffers quit in protest:* William Saletan, "The Gary Bauer Scandal," *Slate,* October 1, 1999, http://slate.msn.com/id/35836/.

*The rumors forced Bauer to call a press conference:* Douglas Kirker, "Bauer Denies Affair Rumor," *Washington Post,* September 29, 1999, www.washingtonpost.com/wp-srv/aponline/19990929/aponline131216_000.htm; Charisse Jones, "Gay Marriage on the Ballot in Eleven States," *USA Today,* October 14, 2004, www.usatoday.com/news/politicselections/2004-10-14-gaymarriage-ballots_x.htm; and Saletan, "Gary Bauer Scandal."

*"Kerry Too Liberal for America":* "Gary Bauer Announces New

Television Campaign in Michigan and Pennsylvania," Press release reprinted by USNewswire.com, September 27, 2004, http://releases.usnewswire.com/GetRelease.asp?id=36937.

"... *given the high rates of disease"*: Gary Bauer, "Why We Must Defend Marriage," American Values, June 16, 2004, www.ouramericanvalues.org/press_release_article.php?id=06160401.

*Alan Keyes*

*Everything seemed to be in place for political success:* "Alan Keyes's Biography," Ambassador Speakers Bureau and Literary Agency, www.ambassadoragency.com/client_profile/cid/164 (accessed May 13, 2005).

... *"eloquently elevating"*: "Who Is Alan Keyes," www.keyes2004.com (accessed April 14, 2005).

... *Keyes griping about Hillary Clinton running for Senate:* Virginia Soto, "It's Alan Keyes vs. Barack Obama," Virginia Soto, About.com, http://chicago.about.com/od/government/a/07050_keyes.htm (accessed April 26, 2005).

... *"dedicated family man"*: "Who Is Alan Keyes?"

*But after his daughter, Maya Marcel-Keyes, publicly announced that she was gay:* "Alan Keyes' Daughter Coming Out," CBS News, February 13, 2005, www.cbsnews.com/stories/2005/02/13/politics/main673732.shtml.

... *tossing her out of the house, and refusing to pay her college tuition:* Sarah Wildman, "Maya's Turn," *The Advocate,* February 13, 2005, http://advocate.com/exclusive_detail.asp?id=02403.

... *called Dick Cheney's daughter Mary ... a "selfish hedonist"*: "Keyes: Cheney's Daughter a Sinner," Associated Press, aired on Fox News, September 1, 2004, www.foxnews.com/story/0,2933,131101,00.html.

*"It was kind of strange that he said it like a hypothetical"*: Marc

Fisher, "When Sexuality Undercuts a Family's Ties," *Washington Post,* February 13, 2005, www.washingtonpost.com/wp-dyn/articles/A20005-2005Feb12.html.

*Rush Limbaugh*

. . . *Rush Limbaugh['s] talk show . . . can boast twenty million "Dittohead" listeners:* Frank Cerabino, "Taking on Rush," *Palm Beach Post,* February 15, 2004, www.palmbeachpost.com/local news/content/news/limbaugh/021504_limbaugh.html.

. . . *only one is a former drug addict:* Tracy Connor, "Rush Limbaugh in Pill Probe," *New York Daily News,* October 2, 2003, www.nydailynews.com/10-02-2003/front/story/122839p-110349c. html; and "Limbaugh Admits Addiction to Pain Medication" CNN, October 10, 2003, www.cnn.com/2003/SHOWBIZ/10/10/rush.limbaugh/.

*Born in Cape Girardeau:* "Rush Limbaugh: Biography," Answers. com, www.answers.com/topic/rush-limbaugh (accessed April 26, 2005).

*A boil on his butt might've literally saved his ass:* Al Franken, "Block That Rush!" *The Nation,* June 1, 2000, www.thenation.com/doc. mhtml%3Fi=20000619&s=franken.

*"If you want a successful marriage":* Scott McCabe, "Rush Announced That He and Marta Were Splitting Up," *Palm Beach Post,* www.palmbeachpost.com; and Scott McCabe, "Limbaugh, Third Wife Divorcing After Ten Years," *Palm Beach Post,* June 12, 2004, page A1, www.palmbeachpost.com/localnews/content/news/limbaugh/cla_rush_0612.html.

*"Why should blacks be heard?":* Jeff Cohen and Steve Randall, "Can a Man Who Has a Problem with People of Color Be a Color Commentator on Monday Night Football?" Common Dreams News Center, May 2, 2000, www.commondreams.org/views/060700-104.htm.

*. . . admitted in court that he was, indeed, hooked on illegal drugs:* Connor, "Rush Limbaugh in Pill Probe," and "Limbaugh Admits Addiction to Pain Medication."

*"Drug use, some might say, is destroying this country":* Rush Limbaugh, on his radio show, October 5, 1995.

## Representative Dick Armey

*Yes, I am Dick Armey:* Ben White and Beth Berselli, "Armey Upsets Gays with Off-Color Joke," *Washington Post,* August 5, 2000, p. A11.

*The enlightened voters of the Twenty-sixth District of Texas:* Pete Winn, "'Friend of the Family' Steps Down," Focus on the Family, December 12, 2001, www.family.org/cforum/feature/a0018890.cfm; and Craig Winneker, "Dick Armey: Is He Really Worse Than Newt?" *Slate,* July 13, 1997: http://slate.msn.com/id/1826/; and Richard L. Berke, "Flurry of Anti-Gay Remarks Has G.O.P. Fearing Backlash," *New York Times,* June 30, 1998, late edition, p. A1.

*. . . he himself was an old pervert:* Miriam Rozen, "The Improbable Rise of Richard Armey," *Dallas Observer,* May 4, 1995.

*. . . even though he never served a day in his life:* Candidate profile from *Congressional Quarterly,* as reprinted on CNN.com, www.cnn.com/ELECTION/1998/states/TX/H/26/dick.armey.html (accessed May 3, 2005).

*Three students publicly claimed that Armey had sexually harassed them:* Rozen, "Improbable Rise of Richard Armey."

## Laura Schlessinger, PhD

*Schlessinger is a licensed counselor:* "Dr. Laura Schlessinger," Biography.com, www.biography.com/search/article.jsp?aid=9542197 &search (accessed April 26, 2004).

*. . . homosexuality is a biological error:* Stop Dr. Laura: A Coalition Against Hate, "Words of Insult," www.stopdrlaura.com/laura/

(accessed April 26, 2005); and Leslie Bennetts, "Diagnosing Dr. Laura," *Vanity Fair,* September 1998.

*"When we have the word 'homosexual'":* Stop Dr. Laura, "Words of Insult," and Bennetts, "Diagnosing Dr. Laura."

*"I pretty much preach, teach, and nag":* Lorenzo W. Milam, "Tell Laura I Love Her," August 23, 1999, www.salon.com/people/feature/1999/08/23/drlaura/.

*. . . Schlessinger became a regular in [Bill Ballance's] bed:* "Bill Ballance," NNDB.com, www.nndb.com/people/789/000063600/ (accessed April 14, 2005).

*In 1975, Ballance snapped some photographs:* "Dr. Laura, How Could You?" Patrizia DiLucchio, *Salon,* November 3, 1998, http://archive.salon.com/21st/feature/1998/11/03feature.html.

*After Dr. Laura sued IEG and lost:* Courtney Macavinta, "Court OKs Nude Dr. Laura Photographs," CNET, November 3, 1998, http://news.com.com/Court+OKs+nude+Dr.+Laura+photos/2100-1023_3-217407.html.

*"I am mystified as to why this eighty-year-old man":* Macavinta, "Court OKs Nude."

## Representative Henry Hyde

*A Roman Catholic:* "Meet Congressman Henry Hyde," http://henryhyde.org/hyde_contents/about/ (accessed April 26, 2005).

*Hyde supported the Defense of Marriage Act;* Issues2000, "Henry Hyde," www.issues2000.org/IL/Henry_Hyde.htm (accessed April 26, 2005); Denise Bernstein and Leslie Kean, *Henry Hyde's Moral Universe: Where More Than Space and Time Are Warped* (Monroe, Maine: Common Courage Press, 1999).

*. . . Henry Hyde led the charge for impeachment proceedings:* "Lead House Manager Henry Hyde's Summation of the Case Against the President," reprinted on Australianpolitics.com, January 16, 1999, www.australianpolitics.com/usa/clinton/trial/1601hyde.shtml.

. . . *Hyde had played Hide Little Hank:* David Talbot, "This Hypocrite Broke Up My Family," *Salon,* September 16, 1998, www.salon.com/news/1998/09/cov_16newsb.html.

. . . *Salon's editorial staff had the tiniest inkling: Salon* editorial, "Why We Ran the Henry Hyde Story," *Salon,* September 16, 1998, www.salon.com/news/1998/09/16newsc.html.

*The whip asked the FBI to open an investigation:* "FBI Will Review House 'Intimidation' Complaint," CNN, September 18, 1998, http://edition.cnn.com/ALLPOLITICS/stories/1998/09/18/hyde.folo/.

*". . . youthful indiscretion":* "Hyde Affair: Resignation Offer Rejected," CNN, September 19, 1998, www.cnn.com/ALLPOLITICS/stories/1998/09/19/hyde.folo/.

. . . *a character witness for men like Joseph Scheidler:* Joe Conason, "Hypocrite of the House," *Salon,* October 5, 1998, http://archive.salon.com/col/cona/1998/10/05cona.html.

. . . *120 counts of criminal predicate: NOW v. Scheidler,* National Organization for Women, www.now.org/nnt/fall-2002/timeline.html (accessed May 3, 2005).

*Senator Phil Gramm*

*A great peril:* Peter Hanson, "The Hatred Behind the Defense of Marriage Act," *University of Washington Daily,* September 30, 1996, http://archives.thedaily.washington.edu/1996/093096/hanson93096.html.

*While he opposed legislation that would make it easier to end life inside the womb:* "Phil Gramm," Issues2000, www.issues2000.org/Senate/Phil_Gramm.htm (accessed April 26, 2005).

*Instead, he applied for five deferments during the Vietnam war:* "Phil Gramm's Skeleton Closet," Real People for Real Change, www.realchange.org/gramm.htm (accessed April 27, 2005).

. . . *"the redneck vote":* Will Saletan, "Slick Philly," *Mother Jones,*

July/August, 1995, www.motherjones.com/news/feature/1995/07/saletan.html.

... *"I'm carrying so much pork, I'm beginning to get trichinosis"*: "Phil Gramm's Skeleton Closet."

*Stiles fronted Gramm $117,000, interest free:* David S. Cloud, "Gramm Deal Questioned," *Congressional Quarterly Weekly Report,* December 5, 1992.

*When Gramm's letters arrived, the prison gates flew open, and Doyle roamed free:* Will Saletan, "Phil's Felon," *Mother Jones,* January 1995, www.motherjones.com/news/feature/1995/07/saletan.html.

... *the state should not legitimize homosexual relationships by legalizing same-sex "marriage":* Phil Gramm, press release, Colorado for Family Values, February 7, 1996.

... *he sank $7,500 of his own money into the movie:* Al Franken, *Rush Limbaugh Is a Big Fat Idiot and Other Observations* (New York: Delacorte Press, 1996), p. 153.


*Representative Helen Chenoweth*

*"I've asked for God's forgiveness, and I've received it":* David Neiwert, "Lives of the Republicans, Part II," *Salon,* September 16, 1998, http://archive.salon.com/news/1998/09/16news.html; and "The Two Faces of Helen Chenoweth," *Religious Freedom Coalition,* www.tylwythteg.com/enemies/helen.html (accessed April 14, 2005).

*Chenoweth's most loyal constituents:* David Neiwert, "God and Country: How the Militia Movement Undermines Separation," Sullivan County, www.sullivan-county.com/id3/militia_sep.htm (accessed April 14, 2005).

*"Regulatory and case law":* Neiwert, "God and Country."

*He also had a mistress named Helen Chenoweth:* Bruce Morton, "Affair Doesn't Dampen Support for Idaho's Chenoweth," CNN,

November 4, 1998, www.cnn.com/ALLPOLITICS/stories/1998/
11/03/election/house/idaho.cd1/.

*"My private life is my own life":* Neiwert, "Lives of the Republicans," and "Two Faces of Helen Chenoweth."


## Reverend Sun Myung Moon

. . . *former president George H. W. Bush delivered a speech:* "Bush Praises Moon as 'Man of Vision,'" *Reuters,* November 25, 1996, as published in *Catholic World News,* www.cwnews.com/news/viewstory.cfm?recnum=3061.

. . . *Moon's minions ran a staff editorial:* "The Massachusetts Example," *Washington Times* editorial, November 19, 2003, www.washingtontimes.com/op-ed/20031118-083536-7321r.htm; and Wayne Madsen, *Counterpunch* "Moon Shadow," January 14, 2003, www.counterpunch.org/madsen01142003.html.

. . . *Moon impregnated a university student, Myung Hee Kim:* "Sun Myung Moon," NNDB.com, www.nndb.com/people/745/000022679/ (accessed April 12, 2005).

. . . *he even gives them explicit instructions in his religious texts:* John Gorenfield, "Hail to the Moon King," *Salon,* June 21, 2004, www.salon.com/news/feature/2004/06/21/moon/.

*Sex before marriage is out of the question:* Unification Church, American Blessed Family Department, and Tparents.org, "Instructions for the Three-Day Ceremony," December 1990, www.tparents.org/library/unification/topics/traditn/3-dayceremony.htm.

. . . *his critics charge that he used soft money to influence:* Bob Fitrakis, "Dark Side of the Moon," *Columbus Alive,* February 24, 2000, www.columbusalive.com/2000/20000224/bob.html.

*In 2003, in a ceremony in a Senate office building:* Gorenfield, "Hail to the Moon King."

# The Silent Majority
## Representative Bill Thomas

*"Any personal failures of commitment"*: "Rep. Thomas Denies Conflict of Interest with Pharmaceutical Industry Lobbyist," CNN, June 27, 2000, http://archives.cnn.com/2000/ALLPOLI TICS/stories/06/27/thomas.letter/.

*He voted for term limits:* "Bill Thomas," Issues2002, www. issues2002.org/CA/Bill_Thomas.htm (accessed April 14, 2002); and Jack Hitt, "The Diddly Awards: Honoring Our Rubber-Stamp Congress, Whose Members Have Found Plenty of Time to Do Squat," *Mother Jones,* September 2002, www.motherjones. com/news/feature/2002/09/diddly.html.

*. . . Bill Thomas graduated from Santa Ana Community College:* "Representative William M. 'Bill' Thomas," Vote-Smart.org, www.vote-smart.org/bio.php?can_id=H0340103 (accessed April 25, 2005).

*Thomas has the fidgety manner of an overgrown boy:* Mark Leibovich, "Bill Thomas, Rep. with a Rep," *Washington Post,* July 27, 2003, www.washingtonpost.com/ac2/wp-dyn?pagename=article &contentId=A51403-2003Jul26.

*. . . has received failing grades by nearly every think tank in town:* "Bill Thomas," and Hitt, "Diddly Awards."

*The article described an "intensely personal relationship":* Vic Pollard, "The Congressman and the Lobbyist," *Bakersfield Californian,* June 25, 2000; "Deborah Steelman Collected Nearly $3 Million from Healthcare Industry Interests with Major Stake in Healthcare Reform," *Public Citizen,* www.citizen.org/congress/ reform/drug_industry/contribution/articles.cfm?ID=936 (accessed April 14, 2005); and Vic Pollard, "Steelman: Intelligent, Ambitious," *Bakersfield Californian,* June 25, 2000.

*"To suggest that I would stoop to an 'inappropriate relationship'":* Jack Hitt, "The Sex in Congress Awards," *Mother Jones,* Sep-

tember/October 2002, www.motherjones.com/news/feature/2002/
09/diddly_05.html.

... *Thomas received nearly $57,000:* Pollard, "Congressman and
Lobbyist," "Deborah Steelman Collected," and Pollard, "Steelman: Intelligent, Ambitious."


### Representative Dan Burton

*"Burton hails from ... Indianapolis":* United States House of Representatives, "Congressman Dan Burton," http://house.gov
(accessed April 14, 2005).

*Like Bill Clinton, whom Burton called "a scumbag":* Daryl Lindsey,
"Dan Burton's Glass House," *Salon,* February 28, 2001, http://
dir.salon.com/politics/feature/2001/02/28/burton/index.html?sid=
1016277; and Charles R. Babock, "Pakistan Lobbyist's Memo
Alleges Shakedown by House Probe Leader," *Washington Post,*
March 19, 1997, www.washingtonpost.com/wp-srv/politics/special/
campfin/stories/cf031997.htm.

... *Burton's politics reflect a little self-hatred:* Russ Baker, "Portrait
of a Political 'Pit Bull,'" *Salon,* December 22, 1998, www.russ-
baker.com/pit%20bull%204.htm; and Jason Vest, "Secret Lives
of the Republicans, Part I," *Salon,* September 11, 1998, http://
archive.salon.com/news/1998/09/11newsb.html.

*Burton's antigay, antieducation, antiminority:* "Dan Burton,"
Issues2000, www.issues2000.org/IN/Dan_Burton.htm (accessed
April 26, 2005).

... *demonstrated his hypothesis with a rifle and a watermelon:*
Lindsey, "Burton's Glass House," and Babcock, "Pakistan Lobbyist's Memo."

... *"Dan Burton was known as the biggest skirt-chaser in the Indiana legislature":* Baker, "Portrait of a Political," and Vest, "Secret
Lives of Republicans."

*She was most embarrassed:* Baker, "Portrait of a Political."

## Senator Strom Thurmond

*"We regard the decisions of the Supreme Court":* Strom Thurmond, *Congressional Record,* 84th Congress Second Session, vol. 102, part 4, March 12, 1956.

*Senator Strom Thurmond was born in 1902:* Strom Thurmond Institute, Clemson University, "Strom Thurmond Biography," www.strom.clemson.edu/strom/bio.html (accessed April 27, 2005); "Thurmond Marks 100th birthday," CNN, December 6, 2002, http://archives.cnn.com/2002/ALLPOLITICS/12/05/thurmond.birthday/; and "Strom Thurmond Dead at 100," CNN, December 17, 2003, www.cnn.com/2003/ALLPOLITICS/06/26/thurmond.obit/.

*. . . fathering a baby out of wedlock:* Diane McWhorter, "Strom's Skeleton," *Slate,* July 1, 2003, http://slate.msn.com/id/2085087/.

*"It's just a carry-over from slavery":* Ken Cummins, "Strom's Secret," *Black Commentator,* 1996, www.blackcommentator.com/21_re_print.html.

## Michael Bowers

*He's got a JD, an MBA, an MS, and BS:* "Michael J. Bowers," Balch and Bingham LLC, www.balch.com/people/details.cfm?id=226 (accessed April 14, 2005).

*The trouble started in 1982:* Laura Douglas Brown, "Bowers v. Hardwick at Fifteen," *Southern Voice,* July 12, 2001, www.sodomylaws.org/bowers/bonews06.htm.

*. . . reversing a job offer to attorney Robin Shahar:* Ruth E. Harlow, "Robin Shahar Takes Her Case to the Supreme Court," *Lambda Legal,* February 28, 1998, www.lambdalegal.org/cgi-bin/iowa/documents/record?record=208; and *Shahar v. Bowers, Appeal from the United States District Court for the Northern District of Georgia,* UScourts.gov, Aug. 1, 1997, www.ca11.uscourts.gov/opinions/ops/19939345.MA2.pdf.

. . . *Bowers publicly admitted that he had committed adultery for ten years:* Linda Feldmann, "Adultery Factor in U.S. Politics," *Christian Science Monitor,* March 25, 1998, http://csmonitor.com/cgi-bin/durableRedirect.pl?/durable/1998/03/25/us/us.2.html.

## Bill O'Reilly

*O'Reilly claims he's the son of a working-class family:* "Bill O'Reilly's Biography," FoxNews, www.foxnews.com/story/0,293,155,00.html (accessed April 27, 2005); and Michael Giltz, "Bill O'Reilly Really Likes You," *The Advocate,* September 17, 2002.

. . . *O'Reilly and Fox filed suit against associate producer Andrea Mackris:* Howard Kurtz, "O'Reilly, Accuser, Air Their Cases," *Washington Post,* October 15, 2004, www.washingtonpost.com/wp-dyn/articles/A34312-2004Oct15.html.

*"You would basically be in the shower":* Mackris v. O'Reilly, Fox News, et al., reprinted by *The Smoking Gun,* October 13, 2004, www.thesmokinggun.com/archive/1013043mackris1.html.

. . . *During the course of this dinner:* Ibid.

. . . *since Defendant was Plaintiff's boss:* Ibid.

*O'Reilly's suit against Mackris:* Howard Kurtz, "Bill O'Reilly, Producer Settle Harassment Suit," *Washington Post,* October 29, 2004, www.washingtonpost.com/ac2/wp-dyn/A7578-2004Oct28?language.

. . . *"scurrilous and scandalous":* Jonathan Wald, "O'Reilly Harassment Charges Lead to Court," CNN, October 21, 2004, http://edition.cnn.com/2004/LAW/10/20/oreilly.suit.

*"And just use your vibrator to blow off steam":* Mackris v. O'Reilly.

## SELF-LOATHERS AND WILY EVADERS
### Representative Ed Schrock

*You're in the showers with them!:* Mike Rogers, "Schrock Faces Accusations: Cancels Congressional Campaign," Blogactive.com,

August 30, 2004, www.blogactive.com/2004/08/schrock-faces-accusations-cancels.html.

*He was six-feet-four, two hundred pounds:* Mike Rogers, "Update: Schrock Ignores Past Sexual Liaisons With Men, Casts Vote for Federal Marriage Amendment," Blogactive.com, audio recordings, September 30, 2004, www.blogactive.com/2004_09_01_blogactive_archive.html.

*Schrock sat on several committees:* "Schrock, Edward," Biographical Directory of the United States Congress, http://bioguide.congress.gov.

*"Uh, hi, I weigh two hundred pounds, I'm six-four":* Rogers, "Update."

*"After much thought and prayer":* Louis Hansen, "U.S. Rep. Schrock Drops Re-election Bid over Allegations," *Virginian-Pilot,* August 31, 2004, reprinted at http://home.hamptonroads.com/stories/story.cfm?story=74982&ran=126361; and Michael D. Shear and Chris L. Jenkins, "Virginia Legislator Ends Bid for 3rd Term," *Washington Post,* August 31, 2004.

*"He is a wonderful congressman and a good personal friend":* Pat Robertson, "Response to U.S. Rep. Ed Schrock's Retirement," press release, September 1, 2004, www.patrobertson.com/Press Releases/edshrock.asp.

## Jeff Gannon (aka James Guckert)

*. . . and his anti–same sex marriage comments:* Howard Kurtz, "Jeff Gannon Admits Past 'Mistakes,' Berates Critics," *Washington Post,* February 19, 2005, www.washingtonpost.com/wp-dyn/articles/A36733-2005Feb18.html.

*. . . a pseudonymous partisan cheerleader:* "A Man Called Jeff," Americablog, February 14, 2005, http://americablog.blogspot.com/2005/02/man-called-jeff.html.

*. . . such family values–oriented Web sites as Hotmilitarystud.com:*
Howard Kurtz, "Online Reporter Quits After Liberals' Exposé,"
*Washington Post,* February 10, 2005, www.washingtonpost.
com/wp-dyn/articles/A12640-2005Feb9.html.

*. . . Gannon had gained access to the White House not as a repre-
sentative of* Talon News: Joe Strupp, "Scott McClellan Reveals
That Gannon/Guckert Got GOPUSA Press Pass," *Editor and
Publisher,* February 18, 2005, www.editorandpublisher.com/
eandp/news/article_display.jsp?vnu_content_id=1000808705;
and Eric Boehlert, "Jeff Gannon's Secret Life," *Salon,* February
15, 2005, http://archive.salon.com/news/feature/2005/02/15/
guckert/index_np.html.

*. . . the only reporter who had access to the infamously leaked CIA
memo:* Kurtz, "Jeff Gannon Admits."

### Representative David Dreier

*A self-proclaimed "Reaganaut":* " 'Reaganauts' Still Hold Sway in
DC," MSNBC News, June 8, 2004, http://msnbc.msn.com/
id/5164599/.

*. . . Mark Cromer, says no one checked out the story:* John Byrne,
"Congressman Who Has Voted Against Gay Rights Believed
Gay; Newspapers Said to Have Deliberately Muzzled Reports on
Gay Issues," *Raw Story,* September 14, 2004, www.bluelemur.
com/index/php?p=293.

*. . . Dreier had been living with a man named Brad Smith:* Doug
Ireland, "The Outing," *LA Weekly,* September 24–30, www.
laweekly.com/ink/04/44/news-ireland.php; and Michael Collins
and Mark Cromer, "Congressman Dreier: Gay and Ashamed,"
Larryflynt.com, www.larryflynt.com/notebook.php?id=88.

*. . . Smith enjoyed a salary:* Ireland, "The Outing."

*Together, Dreier and Smith spent a total of forty-five days abroad:*

John Byrne, "Anti-Gay Rep. Said Gay Visited Twenty-five Countries with Alleged Partner Using Taxpayer Funds," *Blue Lemur,* October 30, 2004, www.bluelemur.com/index.php?p=314.


## Ken Mehlman

*A graduate of Harvard Law School:* "Ken Mehlman," GOP.com, www.gop.com/GOPDirectory/LeaderBio.aspx?ID=8 (accessed April 14, 2005).

*. . . he began bringing gay Republican lobbies (called the Austin 12) into agenda discussions:* "Bush Campaign Mum on Any Openly Gay Staffers," Adrian Brune, *Washington Blade,* May 28, 2004, www.washblade.com/2004/5-28/news/national/bushmum.cfm.

*. . . attempts by the Bush/Cheney campaign to suppress the Mehlman story:* Mike Rogers, "Is He or Isn't He? What the *Washington Blade* Has Not Told You," Blogactive.com, November 30, 2004, www.blogactive.com/2004/11/take-action-is-he-or-isn't-he-what.html.

*Then, mainstream radio talk-show host Randi Rhodes:* Transcript of the Randi Rhodes show, reprinted on Blogactive.com, www.blogactive.com/2004/12/randi-rhodes-on-ken-mehlman-and-gop.html.


## Arthur J. Finkelstein

*"I was sort of sad when I read it":* Raymond Hernandez, "Clinton Attacks Gay G.O.P. Strategist Opposing His Wife as Possibly 'Self-Loathing,'" *New York Times,* April 12, 2005, late edition, p. B3.

*In December 2004, a small, quiet ceremony took place at a home in Ipswich:* Adam Nagourney, "G.O.P. Consultant Weds His Male Partner," *New York Times.* April 9, 2005, late edition, P. A17.

*The man was Arthur J. Finkelstein:* Jenna Russell, "Adviser to GOP Had Gay Wedding," *Boston Globe,* April 10, 2005.

## Dr. Paul Crouch

... *Christians are "little gods":* William Lobdell, "Televangelist Paul Crouch Attempts to Keep Accuser Quiet," *Los Angeles Times,* September 12, 2004, p. A1; and www.myfortress.org/PaulCrouch.html.

... *you are robbing God:* Lobdell, "Televangelist Paul Crouch."

... *claiming he'd been fired after a gay love affair with Crouch:* Ibid.

... *paid Ford $425,000:* John Oswald, "TV Rev. in Gay Sex Scandal," *New York Daily News,* September 14, 2004, www.nydailynews.com/front/story/231669p-198802c.html; and Ted Olson, "Former TBN Employee Alleges Gay Tryst with Paul Crouch," *Christianity Today,* September 13, 2004, www.christianitytoday.com/ct/2004/137/11.0.html.

## Dan Gurley and Jay Banning

... *Gurley, Banning and Co. mailed homophobic flyers:* Mike Rogers, "Tell the RNC Leadership That Gay Bashing Must Stop," Blogactive.com, September 23, 2004, www.blogactive.com/2004_09_01_blogactive_archive.html.

... *he busily attempted to couple with the same sex. His profile on Gay.com:* Mike Rogers, "Gurley Admits: Yes That Was My Gay.com Screenname," Blogactive.com, November 16, 2004, www.blogactive.com/2004/11/gurley-admits-yes-that-was-my-gaycom.html; Lou Chibbaro, Jr., "GOP Officials Announce They're Gay," *New York Blade,* October 15, 2004, www.newyorkblade.com/2004/10-15/news/national/rodgers.cfm.

*Jay Banning was yet another target of Mike Rogers's investigative efforts:* John Byrne, "National Field Director for the Republican Party Sought Unsafe Sex, Multiple Partners Online; Admits to Profile but Can't Recall Content," *Blue Lemur,* November 16, 2004, www.bluelemur.com/index.php?p=428; and John Byrne,

"Chief Financial Officer of Republican National Committee Admits He's Gay, Stays Quiet," *Blue Lemur,* October 9, 2004, www.bluelemur.com/index.php?p=305.

## (Dis)Honorable Mentions
### Jack Ryan
... *sex clubs, whips and chains, cages, and group sex:* "Ex-Wife of GOP Senate Candidate Alleged Sex Club Forays," CNN, June 22, 2004, www.cnn.com/2004/ALLPOLITICS/06/22/ryan.divorce/; "Senate Race Sex Scandal," *Smoking Gun,* June 22, 2004, www.thesmokinggun.com/archive/0622041ryans1.html; and "Sex Scandal Ends Ryan Senate Bid," CBS News, June 25, 2004, www.cbsnews.com/stories/2004/06/25/politics/main626069.shtml.

### Senator Bob Dole
*While married to wife Phyllis:* John Yewell, "The Body Politic," *Metro Active,* February 11–17, 1999, www.metroactive.com/papers/metro/02.11.99/cover/love-political-9906.html; "Divorce Returns to Bite Bob Dole," *New York Daily News,* April 27, 1996, reprinted at www.perkel.com/politics/dole/divorce.htm; and Steve Coz, "Can the *National Enquirer* Sell Respectability—and Papers?" *Slate,* October 12, 1997, http://slate.msn.com/id/1835/.

### Senator Jim Bunn
... *Bunn dumped his wife of seventeen years:* Nigel Jaquiss, "Jim Bunn," *Willamette Week,* March 10, 2001, www.wweek.com/html2/leada1010301.html.

### Representative Mark Foley
*In fact, some political observers call the congressman's homosexuality an "open secret":* "Being Gay in the GOP," *Boston Phoenix*

staff editorial, May 30, 2003, www.bostonphoenix.com/boston/
news_features/editorial/documents/02919063.htm; and Adam C.
Smith, "Don't Ask, Because Mark Foley Won't Tell," *St. Petersburg
Times,* June 1, 2003, www.sptimes.com/2003/06/01/Perspective/
Don_t_ask__because_Ma.shtml.

## Senator Tim Hutchinson

*. . . Hutch was about to file for divorce from his wife of twenty-nine
years:* Suzi Parker, "Shootout Among Arkansas Republicans,"
*Salon,* July 16, 1999, www.salon.com/news/feature/1999/07/16/
hutchinson/; and B. Drummond Ayres, Jr., "Senator Running on
Family Values Has a Tough Race After Divorce," *New York
Times,* April 15, 2002, late edition, p. A14.

## Representative Ken Calvert

*Elected to solicit the services of a prostitute in 1993:* Police report,
Corona Police Department, published at www.croftononline.
com/calvert.JPG; and Susan Lehman, "Monica's Dilemma," *Salon,*
October 1998, www.salon.com/media/1998/10/15media.html.

## Randal David Ankeney

*. . . prosecutors said, Ankeney got her drunk:* "Activist Guilty in
Attempted Assault," Bill Hethcock, *Colorado Springs Gazette,*
July 2002.

*. . . a second girl . . . came forward, charging that Ankeney had
raped her as well:* "GOP Activist Accused of Assaulting Another
Girl," ABC News, Channel 7 (Denver), December 18, 2001,
www.thedenverchannel.com/news/1130885/detail.html.

*Ankeney pleaded guilty but tried to change his mind before he was
sentenced:* Bill Hethcock, "GOP Activist Wants to Withdraw
Guilty Plea," *Colorado Springs Gazette,* September 2002.

### Parker J. Bena

*Bena pleaded guilty to possession of child pornography:* Tim McGlone, "Beach Man Sentenced in Child Porn Case," *Virginian-Pilot,* November 17, 2001; Patrick Califia-Rice, "Topping the News," *Spectator Online,* July 30, 2001, www.spectator.net/1187/pages/1187_news.html.

### Representative Jim Kolbe

*But it's hypocrisy to be a gay Republican:* Adrian Brune, "Wave of Outings Hits Congress," *Washington Blade,* June 18, 2004, http://washingtonblade.com/2004/6-18/news/national/wave.cfm; and Dava Purvis, "Outing Gays Who Sponsor Hate on Capitol Hill," www.rawstory.com/exclusives/dara/outing_gays_washington_blade_716.htm.

## ABOUT THE AUTHOR

When he's not busy defending marriage against those who are defending marriage, journalist Bryan Harris plays an active role in the liberal media conspiracy. His work has appeared in various alternative weeklies and dailies in red states. He has also written for the Poynter Institute for Media Studies and the Associated Press. He currently lives in sin with his girlfriend, Molly, in Louisville, Kentucky. Their dog's name is Gabe and he can catch a Frisbee.

# Progressive Politics
# from Tarcher/Penguin

### THE TRAGEDY OF TODAY'S GAYS
*by Larry Kramer. Foreword by Naomi Wolf,*
*Afterword by Rodger McFarlane*
ISBN: 1585424277

Larry Kramer berates gays for their political indifference and a sexual abandon so reckless that "we are murdering each other"—and offers a radically commonsensical and deeply patriotic survival plan.

### THE UNITED STATES OF WAL-MART
*by John Dicker*
ISBN: 1585424226

An irreverent, hard-hitting examination of the world's largest—and most reviled—corporation, which reveals that while Wal-Mart's dominance may be providing consumers with cheap goods and plentiful jobs, it may also be breeding a culture of discontent.

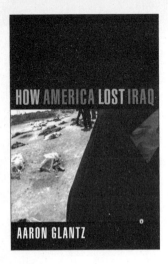

### HOW AMERICA LOST IRAQ
*by Aaron Glantz*
ISBN: 1585424269
A reporter in Iraq shows how the U.S. squandered its early victories and goodwill among the Iraqi people, and allowed the newly freed society to slip into violence and chaos.

### WEAPONS OF MASS DECEPTION
*by Sheldon Rampton and John Stauber*
ISBN: 1585422762
From the authors of *Trust Us, We're Experts!* and *Toxic Sludge Is Good for You!*, here is the first book to expose the aggressive public relations campaign used to sell the American public on the war with Iraq.

### BANANA REPUBLICANS
*by Sheldon Rampton and John Stauber*
ISBN: 1585423424
The bestselling authors of *Weapons of Mass Deception* lay bare how the "right-wing conspiracy," as represented by the national GOP and its functionaries in the media, lobbying establishment, and electoral system, is undermining dissent and squelching pluralistic politics in America.